THE SECRETS OF BEAUTY

The ultimate guide for skincare, Hair care and make-up for beginners

Jane R. Scaife

The Secrets of Beauty

Copyright

About the author

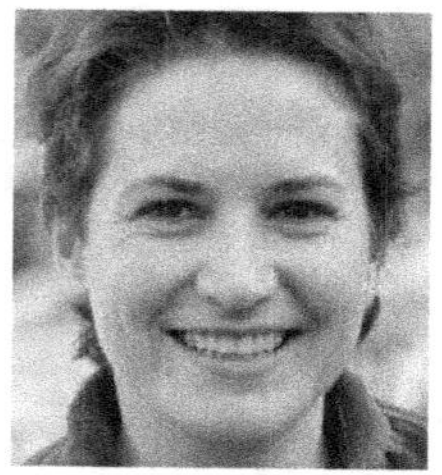

Jane R. Scaife has a wealth of experience in the beauty industry. She's a former magazine editor who has worked for some of the most prestigious beauty publications in the world. She's also a certified beauty therapist and an expert in skincare, haircare, and makeup. She's passionate about helping women to feel beautiful and confident, and she hopes that her book will inspire people to take better care of themselves.

As a beauty guru, Jane Scaife has a lot of advice to share on how to achieve healthy and radiant skin. She's a big believer in the importance of a good skincare routine, and she's always testing new products and treatments. She also emphasizes the importance of a healthy diet and regular exercise. In the book, she shares her top tips for keeping skin looking its best, including using sunscreen every day, drinking plenty of water, and getting enough sleep.

Table of contents

INTRODUCTION

Magnificence is something other than shallow - it's an excursion of self-disclosure and taking care of oneself. With the right items, methods,

The Secrets of Beauty

and schedules, you can accomplish wonderful outcomes and feel your best. In this book, you'll find all the data you want to make a tweaked marvel schedule that works for you. We'll begin by investigating the fundamentals of skincare, including how to distinguish your skin type and pick items that are appropriate for you. Then, we'll continue on toward hair care, with methods for purifying, molding, and styling your hair for greatest sparkle and wellbeing. We'll likewise cover the universe of cosmetics, from picking the right items for your complexion to dominating the most recent patterns and strategies. Looking and feeling your best doesn't need to be a secret. With this book, you'll find a definitive manual for skincare, haircare, and cosmetics. From chemicals and toners to serums and lotions, you'll gain proficiency with the fundamental stages for brilliant skin. You'll likewise find the best items for each skin type, so you can fit your skincare routine to your exceptional necessities.

Your hair is a significant piece of your excellence schedule, and this book takes care of you. Become familiar with the best haircare mysteries, from how to wash and condition your hair to styling tips are most certainly included! From smooth and direct to wavy and wound, you'll become familiar with the most effective ways to style your hair. Find the most recent patterns and exemplary looks that never become dated. In addition, get exhortation on picking the right apparatuses and items for your hair type.

Delightful cosmetics begin with a sound, sparkling composition, and this book has all the data you want to accomplish it. You'll figure out how to make the ideal base, and how to shape and feature like a star. Then, you'll find the specialty of eyeshadow, eyeliner, and mascara, so you can make dazzling ...looks that make your eyes pop. To wrap things up, you'll figure out how to consummate your frown with the best lip items and strategies. You'll leave this book having gained the abilities and information to make any look you want. What's more, the greatest aspect? You'll feel wonderful and certain, regardless of what look you pick.

At last, we'll take a gander at how to make a financial plan accommodating a magnificent schedule that doesn't hold back on quality.

Is it safe to say that you are prepared to find the key to looking and feeling your best? We should begin!

The Secrets of Beauty

CHAPTER 1

SKINCARE 101

Incredible skin isn't simply a consequence of good hereditary qualities or DNA. Your day to day propensities, climate and item decisions will all affect how solid your skin is. As a Skin Specialist, I'm asked inquiries, for example, "how would it be a good idea for me to do my skin?", " I don't have the foggiest idea where to begin" and "what items would be advisable for me to utilize?". There are such countless items available to look over that it can become confusing with regards to where to start. We have illustrated under a beginning stage that can frame the premise of a decent skincare routine for most skin types. On the off chance that you are new to skincare, this straightforward Four Stage Establishment interaction can kick you off on your excursion to extraordinary skin. For further developed healthy skin clients this Four

The Secrets of Beauty

Stage Establishment is the basis on which to develop and include further developed items.

THE FOUR Stages SKINCARE Establishment

1. Purging
2. Toner
3. Exfoliant
4. Saturating/Sunscreen

Stage 1: Purging

Purging eliminates contaminations, soil, sweat and contamination and so on from our skin and gives a perfect surface to our different items to work all the more really. Pick a chemical in light of your skin type eg. Sleek, dry, touchy, rosacea and so forth.

Scrub both morning and night. At night a twofold purge is prescribed to eliminate cosmetics, contamination particles, sweat, and so on. from the skin. In the first part of the day a fast scrub will prepare your skin for the afternoon and permit any cosmetics to sit better on the skin.

Skin Type	Cleanser Type	Suggested Products
Sleek/Skin inflammation/ Breakout inclined	Delicate clean, glue, leave on gel/serum.	As quickly as possible Day to day shedding clean, viewpoint peeling dirt cover, Cosmedix virtue detox scour.
Dry/Mature skin	Velvety exfoliant, delicate scour, leave on gel/serum.	Pronto day to day shedding clean, Cosmedix serum 16.

The Secrets of Beauty

Sensitive/Reactive/Rosacea	Delicate leave on glue, exceptionally delicate clean, peeling serum.	Viewpoint organic product compound veil, Cosmedix resist.
Normal/All Skins	Serum glue, leave on gel/serum.	Quickly everyday shedding scour, Cosmedix unadulterated chemicals.

Step 2: Toner

A toner can have a double reason in your everyday practice - eliminating any extra lingering cleaning agent and rehydrating/adjusting the skin. Gone are the times of unforgiving astringent toners. They have been supplanted with exceptionally successful recipes loaded with skin cherishing fixings. They are an incredible method for adding additional sustenance and supplements to the skin without overcomplicating your daily schedule.

Skin Type	Toner type	Proposed Items
Oily/Acne/Breakout prone	Mist or liquid.	Cosmedix purity balance, Cosmedix

			mystic.
Dry/Mature	Mist liquid.	or	Cosmedix benefits balance.
Sensitive/Reactive/Rosacea	Mist liquid.	or	Cosmedix benefits balance, Cosmedix mystic.
Normal/All Skins	Mist liquid.	or	Cosmedix mystic.

Step 3. Exfoliate

Our skin normally replaces itself at regular intervals. This can dial back to around each 40-50 days as we age. The top layer of our skin is composed of these dead skin cells and despite the fact that our body will normally administer these cells not every one of them are taken out and will quite often adhere to the skin's surface. The outcome can be a form of dead skin cells that can make our skin look dull, dry, and will keep other skincare items from infiltrating and functioning as they should inside the skin. Normal peeling can assist with eliminating these overabundant skin cells. Contingent upon your skin type will rely on how frequently you want to shed.

- Slick skin - up to 2-3 times each week.
- Dry skin - by and large 1 time each week.
- Delicate/Responsive - 1 time each week contingent upon how the skin feels. This step might be skipped in the event that the skin is in a profoundly responsive state.
- Ordinary skin - up to 1-2 times each week.

Skin Type	Exfoliant Type	Suggested Products
Oily/Acne/Br eakout prone.	Gentle scrub, paste, leave	Asap Daily exfoliating

	on gel/serum.	scrub, aspect exfoliating clay mask, Cosmedix purity detox scrub.
Dry/Mature.	Creamy exfoliant, gentle scrub, leave on gel/serum.	Asap daily exfoliating scrub, Cosmedix serum 16.
Sensitive/Reactive/Rosacea	Gentle leave on paste, very gentle scrub, exfoliating serum.	Aspect fruit enzyme mask, Cosmedix defy.
Normal/All skins.	Serum paste, leave on gel/serum.	Asap daily exfoliating scrub, Cosmedix

		pure enzymes.

Step 4. Moisturizer and Sunscreen

The primary capability of a lotion is to hydrate and relax the skin. Skin loses dampness through our current circumstance (sun openness, cooling, air travel) and exercises, (for example, work out, face washing). Lotion ought to be applied each day and night in the wake of purging and conditioning. Lotions have an additional advantage of dynamic fixings to address and assist with adjusting skin conditions.

Skin Type	Moisturizer Type	Products Suggested
Oily/Acne/Breakout prone.	Lotion, light weight gel.	PCA clear skin, aspect sheer hydration,

		Cosmedix shineless.
Dry/Mature	Medium weight lotion, cream.	PCA collagen hydrator, asap ultimate hydration, aspect super moisturizing cream, Cosmedix humidify.
Sensitive/Reactive/Rosacea	Lotion, gel, cream.	Cosmedix rescue, aspect hydra shield, Cosmedix emulsion, Cosmedix hydrate +
Normal/All skins	Lotion, gel, cream.	Asap advanced

		hydrating moisturizer, emulsion.

Sunscreen – maybe the main skin item to utilize! The greatest guilty party of skin maturing is the sun. Any openness to the sun can cause fundamental harm and untimely maturing. Utilizing an ordinary sunscreen (indeed, even in winter!) can go far in forestalling profound kinks, matured skin, and obviously destructive skin malignant growths. Utilizing a base SPF30+ and in a perfect world a SPF50+ on the face and body consistently is an unquestionable requirement. There are a large number of various surfaces, equations and so on for various skin types and inclinations. A few items will consolidate sunscreen and a day lotion in one item - makes it simple to always remember to put your sunscreen on.

The Secrets of Beauty

Skin Type	Sunscreen Type	Suggested Products
Oily/Acne/Breakout prone	Light lotion, spray, gel	Coola Classic Face Organic Sunscreen SPF50, asap CC correcting Cream spf15
Dry/Mature	Cream lotion, spray	Cosmedix Peptide Rich Defense SPF50, Aspect Sun Hydrating SPF50
Sensitive/Reactive/Rosacea	Physical sunscreen, Zinc Oxide and Titanium Oxide based	Colorescience All Calm Clinical Redness Corrector

		SPF50, asap CC Correcting Cream SPF15, Aspect Hydra Shield with Zinc,
Normal/All Skins	Lotion, spray, gel	Coola Classic Face Organic Sunscreen SPF50, Colorescience SunForgettable Total Protection Face Shield SPF50
Body	Lotion, spray, gel	Coola Classic Organic Body Sunscreen

		Spray SPF50, Aspect Envirostat On The Go SPF50

CONSISTENCY IS Critical

Single word of exhortation - consistency is key here; follow these means each and every day and you ought to be headed to accomplishing a solid looking coloring.

5 FACTORS THAT COULD Adversely Influence THE SKIN

You might be taught to accept skin issues influence teenagers and the older, yet issues with the skin can influence people of all ages. Regardless of your age, you should think about how your lifestyle and surroundings may affect your skin's condition.

The following are five factors that might be influencing your skin, and how you could balance the negative.

1. Wintertime Climate

Cold winter weather conditions frequently cause dry skin for some. You might see that your lips feel dried or your skin becomes flaky and bothersome throughout the colder time of year. Skin conditions like psoriasis can be made worse by being exposed to the biting wind, which frequently dehydrates the skin. While wandering outside on a cold and breezy day, give a valiant effort to conceal so your skin isn't uncovered. Make sure to drink plenty of water throughout the winter to stay hydrated. Applying a moisturizer to your body and face may also be beneficial. Use a product that has been tested by a dermatologist. In spite of the fact that you might be enticed to warm yourself by scrubbing down on a virus winter day, utilize warm water all things considered. Your skin may become even more irritated and dry after a hot bath or shower.

2. Pollutants and Dust Exposure

If you work in a dusty environment, your skin may be particularly vulnerable. Your skin may appear dull and clogged with pores if you are exposed to chemicals, pollutants, and dust. Poisons may likewise cause skin inflammation eruptions. A well-thought-out skin care routine is the most effective way to combat the effects of the environment on the skin. To get rid of dirt and grime, wash your face every day and at night. Make sure to utilize tepid water rather than hot. Blackheads and clogged pores can occur if you don't wash your face at the end of the day, so follow your skin care routine carefully.

3. Horrible eating routine

A horrible eating routine isn't sound in any respect, and your food decisions might be influencing your skin. Antioxidant-rich fruits and vegetables are essential to the fight against free radicals that can cause aging of the skin. Moreover, such a large number of desserts and starches might add to skin break out, so limit these in your eating routine. You should think about including cashews and berries in your diet. Zinc-rich nuts and berries may assist in reducing inflammation. Also, cut back on sodium and caffeine in your diet because both can make you more likely to get acne.

4. Absence of Sleep

You may notice that your skin appears dull or is more prone to acne flare-ups if you don't get enough sleep. Absence of rest might make your body produce elevated degrees of cortisol. Cortisol is a pressure chemical, and at undeniable levels, the body and skin are inclined to irritation. You might also notice that sleep deprivation frequently results in dark circles under your eyes. Dilated blood vessels, which frequently occur when you don't get enough sleep, are what give your skin its dark appearance. Take good care of your skin by getting enough sleep each night.

5. Changes in Hormones

Your skin frequently responds to hormonal shifts and changes. Females might see skin inflammation breakouts during their feminine cycle. As you get older and get closer to menopause, dry skin may become more common. Hormonal changes can cause skin problems at various points in your life.

In your skin care routine, remember to be proactive. Purifying, saturating, and eating a solid eating routine might assist with keeping your skin adjusted during hormonal changes.

If you have additional concerns about skin conditions and skin care in general, consult your dermatologist for advice. If over-the-counter products don't work, you may need a prescription.

Common skincare mistakes that everyone makes

If you have acne-prone skin, you know how much trial and error it takes to find the right products. It's just as important to follow the right procedures. You might think these two perspectives are the way to accomplishing your skin objectives, however it doesn't necessarily in all cases end that way. While there are things you might do well, there are a few skincare blotches that come in the method of you getting clear skin. We are here to inform you of the most common skincare blunders you make and the reasons why you should avoid them.

1. Overwashing your face.

Washing your face twice a day is more than sufficient, contrary to popular belief. A lot of people make the skincare error of washing their face too much. If you wash your face too much, it loses its natural oils and becomes overly dry. Your glands go into overdrive as a result, producing more sebum and oils. The sebum stops up your pores and results in breakouts. To try not to commit this skincare error, decide on a cleaning agent that is delicate yet saturating. Because it cleanses without drying your skin, a brightening cleanser is ideal.

2. Constantly Touching your face.

This is the most common skincare mistake if you have acne-prone skin! Every day, we move around and our hands carry germs and dirt. Contacting your face continually moves this soil onto your skin. This may aggravate existing breakouts and aggravate new ones. To stay away from this skincare botch, trying not to contact your face constantly is ideal. Furthermore, it is additionally essential to continuously make sure to clean up prior to applying skincare items.

3. SPF is not used.

Stop making this skincare mistake now if you haven't started using SPF yet! The sun's rays can cause severe skin damage. Your skin gets very dry if you get too much sun. This causes an excess of oils and sebum to be produced, which may aggravate your pimples. Use a moisturizer with an SPF to avoid this common skincare blunder. This will keep your skin hydrated and furthermore safeguard it from sun harm. For continuous sun protection, remember to reapply your sunscreen every two to three hours.

4. Utilizing brutal exfoliators.

Scouring your face every once in a while is exceptionally gainful for the skin. However, using the wrong product to scrub your face can cause severe damage to the skin. A great many people actually commit this skincare error and choose Do-It-Yourself or physical exfoliators. The skin is damaged by these physical exfoliators, which cause microtears and irritation. They may aggravate and aggravate your existing pimples. Chemical exfoliators can help you avoid making this common skincare mistake. Chemical exfoliants also aid in the removal of dead skin cells and deep cleansing of the skin. In any case, they are extremely delicate and assist with advancing cell turnover in the skin. A vitamin C serum is one of the best options for this, especially for beginners. The cell reinforcement properties of L-ascorbic acid assist with advancing solid cell turnover and lift its recovery. Your skin will feel extremely soft and appear brighter as a result.

5. Applying makeup for sleep.

We're certain you've known about the legend that cosmetics cause skin break out. Indeed, the time has come to expose this legend and figure out reality! Utilizing cosmetics consistently doesn't make your skin break out, but not taking it off appropriately brings about disturbing the skin. One of the most common skincare faux pas is to wear makeup to bed. It is essential to thoroughly remove makeup after wearing it for the entire day. Not eliminating your cosmetics makes your pores get stopped up and doesn't allow your skin to relax.

Use gentle micellar waters to remove your makeup to avoid making this skincare error.

Micellar water is designed to be gentle on the skin and removes makeup with just one swipe. You can also double cleanse if your skin is prone to acne. After using micellar water to remove your makeup, use a cleanser. This will guarantee that your skin is spotless! Skincare is personal. It varies from individual to individual and even between skin types. The products from the Garnier line can help you develop the ideal skincare routine. So the time has come to adjust your skincare routine and try not to commit these normal skincare errors to accomplish the unmistakable skin of your fantasies!

TIPS TO REMEMBER WHEN CHOOSING A SKINCARE PRODUCT

You might be curious about how to select the ideal skincare products for your skin. With so many choices available, it can be overwhelming, but there are a few things to keep in mind.

I.   First, determine whether you have combination, dry, oily, or sensitive skin.

The Secrets of Beauty

This will assist you with reducing the items that are ideal for you. Furthermore, focus on the fixings in the items. For hydration and anti-aging benefits, look for ingredients like retinol and hyaluronic acid. Products that contain irritating fragrances or harsh chemicals should be avoided.

II.   Secondly, you should look for products that are non-comedogenic, which means that they won't clog your pores.

III.   Thirdly, remember to search for items that are affordable for you. To achieve great results, you do not need to spend a lot of money.

Now that we've covered a portion of the nuts and bolts, what is it that you need to zero in on next in your skincare schedule? Could it be said that you are searching for items to assist with explicit worries, similar to scarcely discernible differences or skin inflammation? Or on the other hand perhaps you're keen on making a more customized everyday practice for your one of a kind requirements?

The Secrets of Beauty

CHAPTER 2

CARE ON THE HAIR

It's vital to comprehend that the hair and scalp are living organs that should be really focused on appropriately. Numerous oil glands and hair follicles can be found on the scalp in particular. It is essential to keep the scalp clean and free of buildup because the health of the hair is directly linked to the health of the scalp. Additionally, the hair itself must be regularly cleaned and conditioned.

What is meant by "hair type?"

Hair type ordinarily alludes to the state of an individual's hair. Straight, wavy, curly, or coily hair are all possible.

One Trusted Source article from 2020 says that hair has two structures:

- The hair shaft or the hair strand itself.
- The hair follicle.

The Secrets of Beauty

The hair shaft comprises various layers, including the cortex, the encompassing cells, and, in thicker hair, a focal medulla.

According to a 2017 study by Trusted Source, a person's hair is shaped by the shape of their hair follicle. For instance, curly hair has hair follicles shaped like an S. A person's hair follicle shape is influenced by genetic factors.

What kinds of hair exist?

Hair shape alludes to the level of waviness of an individual's hair. One survey articleTrusted Source takes note of that various analysts have utilized different hair shape arrangement frameworks in their examination about hair. Some, for instance, have used labels like:

- stick straight
- straight wavy
- big curls
- small curls Some hairstylists like to divide hair into four categories based on its shape.

However, neither medical nor scientific research make use of this classification system.

Hairstylists use the following categorization system:

Hair Type	Shape
Straight Hair	1a: Very straight, fine or thin texture. 1b: Straight with some bends. 1c: Straight with some coarser texture.
Wavy Hair	2a: Wavy and fine. 2b: Wavy with a slightly more defined S-shape. 2c: Wavy with well-defined S-shaped waves.

Curly Hair	3a: Loose curls 3b: Tight and springy curls 3c: An S or Z shape that springs back into shape when stretched
Coil Hair	4a: Loose coils 4b: Zig-zagging coils

The number of hairs on a person's head is referred to as their density. The more hairs an individual has, the higher that individual's hair thickness.

The thickness of the hair strands is referred to as its structure. An individual's hair can be:

- Fine
- Medium
- Coarse

As indicated by the World Trichology Society (WTS), hair thickness shifts relying upon the individual. Hair is finer on some people than on others. The WTS also notes that as a person gets older, their hair fibers become shorter and finer.

Porosity: A person's hair's ability to absorb moisture is measured by its porosity. The amount of holes or tears in the cuticle layer determines the porosity of the hair. The hair's outermost layer, the cuticle, serves to shield the hair from damage.
Hair is naturally porous, according to a 2015 article published by Trusted Source. However, bleached or chemically treated hair has a higher percentage of pores than untreated hair.
To allow their hair to recover, some people may find it helpful to avoid intense heat and chemical treatments.

The American Academy of Dermatology (AAD) recommends the following general hair care tips for individuals to try:
- **Shampoo**: Shampoo the hair as often as necessary. This will commonly be the point at which the hair becomes sleek,

which can occur at various rates for various individuals. Those with slick skin and hair might have to cleanser on a more regular basis. Apply the shampoo solely to the scalp.

- **Condition**: After each shampoo, a person should use a conditioner. Focus the conditioner on the tips of the hair.
- **Dry**: Individuals can either envelop their hair with a towel and let it air dry or utilize a blow-dryer on the most minimal setting. Compared to natural drying, blow-drying can cause more damage to the hair. In any case, there is examination to propose that utilizing a blow-dryer a ways off of 15 centimetersTrusted Source and moving it persistently can make less harm to the hair than air drying.
- **Brush**: Using a comb with wide teeth, brush the hair when it is still damp.

Note: Individuals ought to choose their cleanser and conditioner in light of their hair type.

On the off chance that potential, they ought to attempt to restrict:

- **Extensions and weaves:** Wear lightweight weaves and extensions whenever possible. Hair loss, or traction alopecia, can occur when hair is worn tightly pulled back.
- **Chemical hair treatment**: Individuals ought to attempt to leave some between variety final details. They should also try to get one treatment at a time. This is on the grounds that extremely treated hair is more inclined to breakage.
- **Drying the hair utilizing a towel**: This can pull or turn the hair, making it snap. It can also ruffle the cuticles of the hair.

Instructions for styling straight hair

There is some evidence to suggest that straight hair is more likely to carry sebum than curly hair is. Sebum is an oily, waxy substance produced by the skin. This implies that individuals with straight hair might be bound to get sleek hair than those with curlier hair.

Hence, individuals with straighter hair might wish to keep away from the exorbitant utilization of specific hair items. These are some:

Oils, such as olive, coconut, and jojoba oil Oil-based styling products Leave-on products People with straight hair may also wish to wash their hair more frequently. Any hair product that is labeled for dry hair

A 2015 article published by Trusted Source suggests that people with straight hair may require more gentle hair care. This could include:

Using gentle shampoos, blow-drying the hair with a towel, brushing or combing the hair, and following the care instructions for curly hair. Brushing the hair too much can damage the definition of the curls. Consequently, individuals with wavy hair might have to trial to track down the perfect proportion of brushing for their hair.

Some other consideration tips for wavy hair include:

- Decreasing cleanser utilization
- Air drying or utilizing a diffuser on a blow-dryer
- Keeping away from thick brushes and brushes
- Keeping away from heat styling devices

Certain individuals may likewise wish to utilize hair mousses and gels that are planned for wavy hair to keep up with twist definition.

How to take care of black hair The AAD recommends the following methods for black hair:

- Washing the hair something like one time each week
- Utilizing conditioner at each wash
- Staying away from excessively close meshes, cornrows, or winds around
- Utilizing a hot oil treatment fortnightly

- Utilizing heat safeguarding items before heat styling

Additionally, weaving or applying extensions should be done with caution. They might want to try the following to protect their hair:
before getting a weave or extension, making sure their hair is clean and free of hair products, like hair spray.
Utilizing conditioner to assist with keeping the hair solid.
if at all possible, going to a professional hairstylist.
maintaining a clean scalp with a gentle shampoo. Using water-based gels and moisturizers to protect the hair's edges. Tight hairstyles can also cause traction alopecia, which causes hair loss. Individuals might wish to think about offering the hair a reprieve following 2-3 months of wearing a weave or expansion.

Washing, styling, and other ways to take care of Black hair can help prevent damage, dryness, and fragility. There are numerous ways of keeping the hair solid and hydrated while lessening the gamble of breakage. In this book, we investigate a few qualities of Dark hair, how to really focus on it, and choices for styling.

Characteristics that can impact care

Dark hair is different, with a scope of surfaces and thicknesses. It may have loosely or tightly coiled curls and a curly or spiral shape. The shape of the hair follicle causes this. Straight hair is produced by a round hair follicle, while curly hair is produced by a curved hair follicle.

There are a few vital contrasts between Dark hair and different sorts. The following characteristics may have an impact on hair care:

Width of the cuticle: Every human hair has a protective outer layer known as a cuticle. Research from 2015 Believed Source takes note of that Dark hair has a more slender fingernail skin layer than other hair types, and that implies that strands might break all the more without any problem.

Density in general: There are 90,000 hair follicles in Black hair compared to 120,000 in white hair on average for people of African descent. Therefore, balding might be more perceptible, and an individual's scalp might be simpler to see.

Dryness: To keep the skin and hair hydrated, the scalp produces sebum. This slick substance moves from the scalp along the hair shaft, fixing in dampness. The cycle happens all the more effectively when the hair is straight, and wavy hair can be inclined to dryness.

The most effective method to really focus on Dark hair

There are numerous ways of moving toward hair care, and those that safeguard against harm and add dampness can keep delicate or dry hair sound. If any of these concerns you, you might try:

Washing week by week: Washing tightly coiled hair less frequently than once per week is suggested by the American Academy of Dermatology (AAD). Care products and some sebum can be removed from the hair and scalp by washing more frequently, which may dry them out. Washing one's hair more frequently may be necessary for people who have scalp conditions like dandruff or seborrheic dermatitis. A dermatologist might suggest washing two times per week, for instance. The decision of cleanser is likewise significant. Sulfates, a harsh ingredient in some regular and anti-dandruff shampoos, can strip natural oils from the hair and dry it out, making it harder to comb and more likely to break. Search for delicate, saturating shampoos, and utilize a conditioner with each wash, ensuring that the conditioner covers the finishes of the hair. Massage the scalp gently while washing. Instead of rubbing, use a towel to pat the hair dry.

Conditioning in depth: As well as utilizing a conditioner with each wash, an individual could attempt a profound molding or oil treatment a few times per month. This adds dampness to the hair. Apply a deep conditioner or a natural oil, like jojoba, to the hair and scalp after you've shampooed. Enclose the hair with a warm towel and surrender it for 30 minutes. Choose an oil that melts at body temperature when using it. This makes it unnecessary to heat the oil beforehand.

An individual could have to investigation to track down the right oil for their hair, however a few choices include:

- Jojoba oil.
- Shea margarine or shea spread oil.
- Emu fat.

Combing while the hair is still damp

Curly hair is prone to tangles and can break when brushing. Therefore, when the hair is dry, it is best not to comb it. Instead:

Apply a lotion or a leave-in conditioner while the hair is wet.

- Section off the hair into sections.
- Use light strokes and a wide-toothed or detangling comb to comb through each section, concentrating first on the ends of the hair.
- Move up the hair shaft gradually until every section is untangled.

If the hair is not already damp, it can be dampened with a water-filled spray bottle.

- Diminishing grinding during rest
- Development during rest can rub the hair and cause harm. Additionally, a few textures can ingest dampness from the hair and scalp.

To stay away from these issues, it very well might be smart to:

- Eliminate any solid grasp groups before bed.

- Utilize a smooth, silk or silk hair wrap to decrease erosion.
- Utilize a silk or silk pillowcase.

Ideas and advice for styling Every hair type eventually develops split ends. Managing the closures of the hair consistently can keep it solid and assist it with becoming out. Beyond this initial level of upkeep, a person might try:

Heat styling

Intensity can make the way for a great many styles. Waves and loose curls can be created with heated rollers and curling irons. A heated straightener could also be tried. However, it's important to keep in mind that heat can dry out the hair and cause damage to it over time.

In the event that an individual chooses heat styling, it can serve to:
- Utilize ceramic covered apparatuses.
- Utilize the most minimal intensity setting.
- Hold off until the hair is dry and clean.

- Apply an intensity security item.
- At most, use the heated tool once per week.

Heat damage can be minimized by taking these steps, but it can still happen.

Braids

The shape, style, and complexity of braided hairstyles can vary greatly. An individual could have straightforward meshes for a day or all the more firmly woven interlaces for quite a long time. However, traction alopecia is a condition in which excessively tight braids can pull on the scalp, increasing the risk of breakage, irritation, and hair loss.

Footing alopecia happens when incessant strain on the hair makes it drop out. It can be reversed if the person gets treatment early, but the hair won't grow back if they wear tight styles for a long time.

Low-tension styles that don't pull on the scalp should be used for traction alopecia treatment. If braiding is causing pain, stop the stylist and keep any braids as loose as possible. Likewise, redirecting interlaces consistently can decrease pressure on the scalp. Try not to protect twists with elastic groups or groups that have a metal join.

Locs

Getting locs includes locking, winding, or matting the hair into rope-like strands, which might be thin or thick. Locs cannot be undone and take time to create. They additionally require extraordinary support to hold them back from unwinding. Before getting locs done, it's a good idea to talk to a stylist about how to keep them in good shape.

Chemical treatments like perms and relaxers straighten the hair permanently until it grows out. The hair may gradually weaken as a result of these treatments, and the likelihood of hair breakage increases with each treatmentTrusted Source. Synthetic relaxers can harm the hair and scalp whenever applied inaccurately. Always have these treatments done in a salon by a trained stylist.

As the hair grows, chemical treatments need to be changed every two to three months. New treatment ought to simply be applied to new hair development.

What is Normal Hair Development?

The predominance of white magnificence norms in the US and all through a significant part of the world has brought about bigoted discernments and generalizations about Dark hair. Some Black people, for instance, are not permitted to wear their hair naturally, in braids, or in locs, at work because they are thought by racists to be unprofessional.

Another instance of discrimination occurred in 2018 when a student in Louisiana was expelled from class for wearing braids. Additionally, some people mistakenly believe that locs indicate a lack of hygiene.

In 2020, an examination of four examinations observed that People of color with regular haircuts were less inclined to be suggested for a prospective employee meeting than either People of color with straight hair or white ladies with wavy or straight hair.

There is right now a continuous restoration of the regular hair development, which started during the 1960s. It combats related bias and encourages Black people to wear natural hairstyles.

The Creating a Respectful and Open Workplace for Natural Hair Act, or CROWN Act, was enacted in 2019 and makes it illegal for an employer to discriminate against an employee on the basis of their hair. In any case, bias perseveres, and in many states, hair-based separation is as yet lawful.

Additionally, many doctors lack knowledge of textured hair. 68% of Black female participants in a 2014 study told Trusted Source that their doctor did not seem to understand Black hair. Because of this, it might be hard for people to get advice about things like hair loss, which can hurt their self-esteem and their mental health. To ensure that the requirements of each and every one of their patients and clients are met, it is essential for all hairstylists and doctors to become familiar with Black hair care. Dark hair is assorted and flexible. Firmly snaked hair can be inclined to dryness and breakage, so treating the hair delicately and supporting the degree of dampness is vital to keeping it solid.

Be mindful of items, medicines, or styles that draw on the scalp or debilitate the hair. Consult a dermatologist or other doctor who knows a lot about Black hair care if you notice that your hair is getting weaker, thinner, or shedding a lot.

Care instructions for thick hair Individuals with thick hair may benefit from using products with a higher density, such as:

- Hair gels.

- Hair margarines.
- Hair veils, for example, avocado hair covers.
- Thicker oils, for example, coconut oil.

Moreover, individuals with more prominent hair thickness might find it advantageous to utilize brushes that are intended for thick hair. Because they have fewer spokes than other brushes, these brushes make it easier to remove knots without damaging the hair.

Care Directions for Flimsy Hair

There is narrative proof to propose that denser hair items, like oils and spreads, can burden more slender hair. As a result, people who have thin hair might want to stay away from these products.

Additionally, people who have shorter hair may gain from:

- Employing dry shampoo.
- Regularly washing the hair.

- Concentrate conditioner application only on the hair's ends.

Hair loss is estimated to be between 50 and 150 hairs per day, according to the WTS. This can happen when you brush, comb, or wash your hair. Some people, on the other hand, lose more hair than they can grow. There are numerous causes for this to occur. One normal reason is androgenetic alopecia. This is a hereditarily foreordained condition that affects around 50%Trusted Wellspring of individuals. Males experience hair loss at the temples and crown of the head. Crown hair loss can occur in females. Females may also experience hair loss as a result of the following conditions:

Polycystic ovary syndrome A side effect of birth control pills Thyroid issues A person should see a doctor if:

- Experience unexpected going bald.
- Foster uncovered patches.
- Lose clusters of hair.

- Experience tingling and consuming sensations on the scalp.

Is it preventable?

Some recounted proof proposes that individuals can utilize specific shampoos, rejuvenating ointments, and dietary enhancements to thicken the hair. However, there is no scientific evidence to suggest that taking care of your hair can stop it from thinning.

All things considered, an individual can go to lengths to assist with forestalling certain purposes of balding. like foothold alopecia. Everybody's hair is somewhat unique. Hair can be straight, curly, coily, or wavy, and each type of hair needs different care.

Even though some people experience hair loss, if they are concerned, they should talk to a doctor.

Hair loss can be caused by both aging and genetics. The treatments that work best depend on the root cause of hair loss. Supplements, medicated ointments, and modifications to one's lifestyle are options.

How To Stop Balding?

Balding is a worry for certain individuals. Various methods and treatments may assist in strengthening or regrowing hair, depending on the cause of hair loss. This book contains a few ways to forestall balding and ways of regrowing hair.

Diet

Adjusting diet can meaningfully affect hair development and hair wellbeing.

Diet changes can include:
Eating additional protein

A 2017 studyTrusted Source discovered that few members encountering going bald had low protein and amino corrosive admissions. To determine whether nutritional deficiencies are linked to hair loss, additional research is required. The Mediterranean diet's herbs and vegetables were linked to a lower risk of male pattern baldness, or androgenetic alopecia, according to a 2017 study published in the Archives of Dermatological Research.

Keeping away from crash eats less carbs

Exceptionally low calorie diets can deny the group of fundamental supplements, including those vital for sound hair, like protein, unsaturated fats, and zinc. Most of the time, crash diets don't help people lose weight for good. A 2019 literature review conducted by Trusted Source found that people who lose body cell mass as a result of a low-calorie diet can experience hair loss. This can lead to brief hair loss.

Treatments and supplements

Some treatments and supplements may aid in the prevention or reduction of hair loss. taking supplements for a multivitamin. Concentrates on going back quite a long while proposing nutrients assist with forestalling balding. The role that various vitamins and minerals play in preventing hair loss was the subject of a review published in Dermatology and TherapyTrusted

Source in 2019. The job of nutrients and minerals in balding remaining parts muddled. On the other hand, vitamin deficiency may increase the likelihood of hair loss. Vitamins and minerals that may be of assistance include:

- Vitamin B
- Vitamin D
- Iron
- Vitamin A
- Vitamin C
- Vitamin E should all be discussed with a doctor before taking a multivitamin supplement.

All or most of the recommended daily doses of each vitamin and mineral are found in the best products in a single dose. Dietary supplements, on the other hand, are not subject to the same level of FDA regulation as prescription drugs. Supplements can be analyzed for quality and provided with a Certificate of Analysis (COA) by third-party businesses like NSF, USP, ConsumerLab, or the Banned Substances Control Group (BSCG). Nonetheless, supplements don't need outsider checking to be offered to people in general. An individual might need to pick dietary enhancements that have been checked by an outsider organization.

Assuming going bald drug

A few meds for forestalling going bald are accessible. Minoxidil, applied topically, is the most common treatment for androgenetic alopecia in both men and women, according to a 2019 review of studies byTrusted Source. Rogaine, which can be purchased over the counter (OTC), contains minoxidil, which is the active ingredient. According to the review, doctors may use minoxidil to treat other causes of hair loss, like chemotherapy. According to the review's authors, minoxidil could benefit from additional research. Another treatment for scalp hair loss is Propecia, a prescription medication. It can be applied topically or taken orally. A 2021 clinical trialTrusted Source found that an effective finasteride splash arrangement essentially further developed the hair count of 323 guys with design sparseness.

The Secrets of Beauty

CHAPTER 3

COSMETIC TIPS AND TRICKS

Assuming you've never utilized cosmetics, it may very well be very scary to begin with. There are numerous makeup techniques, colors, shades, tools, and products. This is ordinary. It's completely acceptable not to know where to begin! You can learn a lot about makeup, but it's perfectly normal to feel overwhelmed when you first start. Keep reading to discover makeup 101 for beginners and where to begin. The power of makeup cannot be denied; Our favorite beauty products help us achieve the looks we love, highlight our favorite features, and embody our individual definitions of beauty. The best makeup routines enable modern women to boost their confidence and face the world head-on, regardless of the day's events. With regards to cosmetics, capable application can have a significant effect. The proper application of your favorite cosmetics and the appropriate amount of makeup can accomplish two things: assist you with accomplishing the magnificence look you hunger for, and assist you with capitalizing on your cosmetics.

Are you looking for natural makeup that lasts all day and makes your skin look radiant? Figure out how to put on your cosmetics with these significant excellence tips. This breakdown of makeup steps and advice will help you create a flawless look that you can be proud of, from applying liquid foundation to using gel eyeliner. Applying primer should always be your first step when applying makeup that will last and look beautiful. Primer helps to prepare the skin, fills in wrinkles and fine lines, creates a clean palette for your makeup, and provides a better base layer, extending the wear time of your makeup. The primer you select ought to be oil-free and light.

Moves toward Put on Cosmetics

As we referenced previously, there isn't just a single method for putting on your cosmetics, and there aren't cosmetics steps that are firmly established. In any case, we can give you a breakdown of the means that work for us here in the Colorescience group. We took the time to ensure that this makeup application sequence makes the most sense and will help you achieve a stunning makeup look!

STEP 1: MOISTURIZER

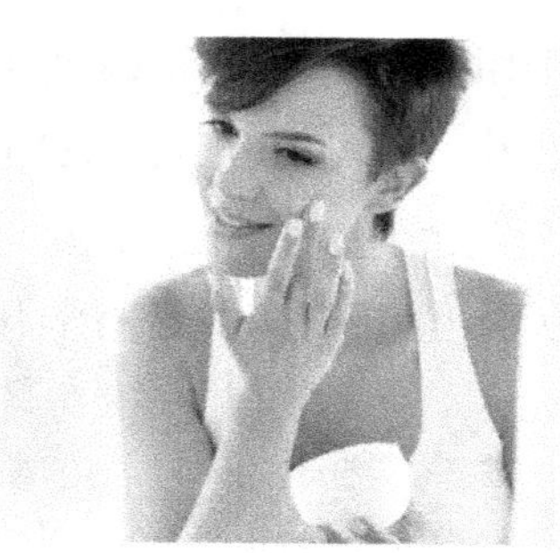

Make use of a high-quality moisturizer to prepare your skin before applying makeup. Picking the right sort of cream is a critical piece of the riddle. Let's take a look at the various kinds you can use, arranged in order of lightness to heaviness:

Eye Mists: These are water-based treatments that might also have fragrances or vitamins that help the skin look better. Facial dogs aren't intended to return the dampness to your skin, yet they can be a useful instrument for keeping a dewy look the entire day. Basically spritz over the course of the day when your skin is feeling dry.

The Secrets of Beauty

Serums: This solution is light and easy to absorb by the skin. Serums designed to address specific issues come in a wide variety. A few serums assist you with saturating the skin to forestall wrinkles, while others contain fixings that might add brilliance to a dull coloring.

Lotions: The most common type of moisturizer, lotions can be beneficial to a wide range of skin types. Choose lotions that say they are "non-comedogenic"; these items are intended to try not to obstruct the pores.

Creams: A cream moisturizer might be in order if your dry skin needs more help. This solution can hydrate excessively dry complexions and is thicker and heavier. Day creams can be utilized as a base under your cosmetics, yet night creams are intended to provide your skin with an additional portion of dampness while you rest. Apply prior to stirring things up around town, and in the first part of the day you'll be welcomed with delicate, graceful skin.

Oils: Assuming you want further saturation, think about oils. People who have dry, sensitive, or normal skin may benefit greatly from using certain oils. However, oil-moisturizing products should be avoided if you suffer from acne or require oily skin-specific makeup.

How to Use the Moisturizer

Squirt a tiny dollop onto your fingers, about the size of a quarter. First, apply the moisturizer to your forehead. start from the focal point of your face, then move outwards and up. Then, do a similar beginning at your nose, spreading the lotion across your cheeks. To keep the moisturizer from clogging your pores, make sure to rub it into your skin evenly. Whenever you've applied enough cream, tenderly focus on it utilizing circles, and give it a couple of moments to dry prior to moving onto the subsequent stage.

STEP 2: PRIMER

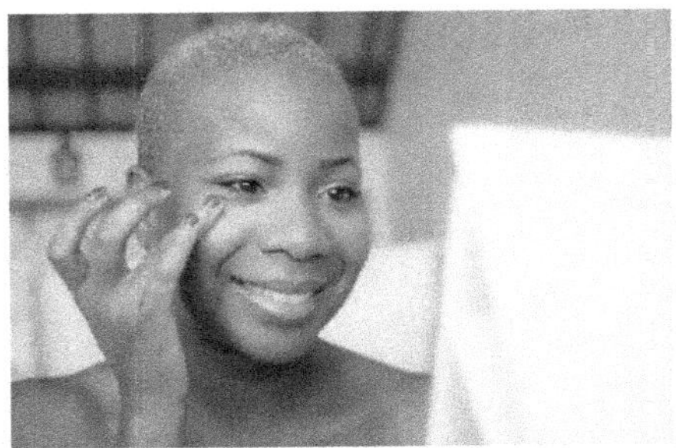

Now that your skin is well moisturized, prep your face with primer. Whether you're planning on applying a light coat of foundation or a full face of makeup, primer is an important first step. Using primer under your makeup will make your look last longer.

So what exactly is primer?

Think of primer as a base for your foundation or face makeup that will help it go on smoother and last longer. Primers are silky smooth gels and creams that fill in the lines and pores on your face, smoothing out uneven textures and creating the ideal canvas for your makeup.

How To Apply Your Primer?

Begin by squeezing a small amount onto your fingertips, or onto your preferred makeup brush or sponge.

Pro Tip: A little bit goes a long way. Start with a dime-sized amount of primer in the center of your face, and slowly work it out towards your cheeks, forehead, and chin.

If you want to apply primer to the sensitive skin around your eyelids (and keep that smokey eye looking professionally applied all day long), be sure to find a dedicated product for this area of the face. Our eyelids can collect grease throughout the day, causing a "creased" look in eyeshadow. If your eyelids are oily and you apply eyeshadow or eyeliner without primer, application may prove to be patchy and uneven.

STEP 3: LIQUID FOUNDATION

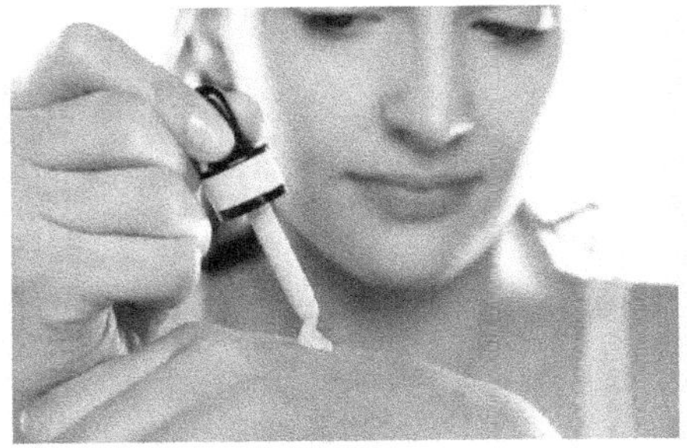

When it comes to foundation, finding the perfect shade for your skin is priority number one. The right shade of foundation can make all the difference. So how do you go about picking? Test foundation colors against your jawline. After applying, if the foundation disappears without any sort of blending, you've found your true match. This may take a bit of trial and error, but taking the time to pick the right shade is crucial.

After you've selected a product, consider the tools you'll use to apply it. Some women prefer to use their fingers, while others opt for beauty tools like brushes and sponges. If you're looking for a light coverage look, your fingers may prove to be the right applicator; however, never touch your face without thoroughly washing your hands, and be sure to wash them after application—you don't want to find your makeup handprints all over the house. For a more full-coverage look, opt for an applicator brush or beauty blender.

Application of Liquid Foundation

Start from the center of your face and blend the liquid foundation outwards. As you sweep your foundation across the skin, be sure to buff it in. Some women like to stipple a damp sponge over their foundation to help ensure it gets into those lines and creases, which can create a smoother, more even texture. Certain types of makeup brushes are also great for buffing foundation into the skin.

STEP 4: CONCEALER

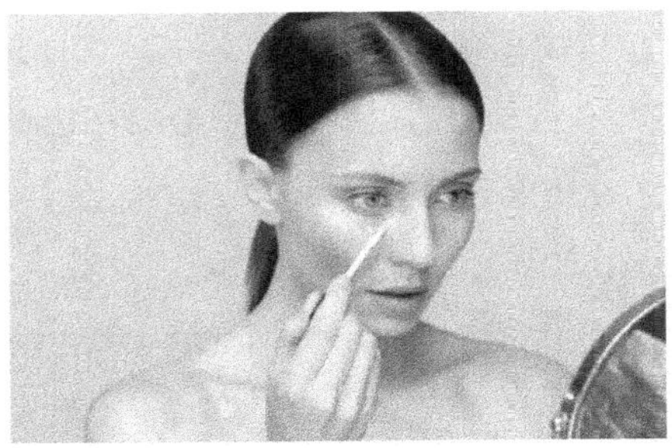

There are two main categories of concealer: liquid and stick/compact.

- **Liquid concealer** is best for the times you want light coverage over a large area of your face. Liquid concealer also works well for those looking to create a light finish, especially in areas of wrinkles, like around the eyes and mouth.

- **Stick and compact concealers** are well-suited for heavier coverage on smaller, more specific areas of the face.

Picking the Color of Your Concealer

It's wise to invest in two shades of concealer. One should be very similar to your skin tone, and can be used to cover dark spots, pimples, and other facial blemishes. The other should be lighter than your skin tone, and can be used to highlight certain areas of the face or add clarity to your makeup look.

Note: Some women prefer to apply concealer before liquid foundation. The order of these two steps is truly a matter of preference—and trial and error. Try out both and discover which method works best for creating a smooth, radiant finish on your skin. However, when using powder foundation alone, always apply concealer first.

Where to Apply Concealer

To reduce the appearance of dark under-eye circles and create a glowing, bright look, apply light concealer beneath the eyes with a damp sponge or makeup brush, and consider using a dark circle cream. If you're using a concealer to minimize the appearance of blemishes, apply directly to problem areas. To highlight your face using a liquid or cream concealer, place small dots in the following areas:

I. Horizontally over the center of your forehead.
II. Down the center of your nose.
III. Under your eyes.
IV. In a curving arch at the top of your chin, just under your bottom lip.
V. Gently blend it into the surrounding skin, and always be sure to cover with a foundation or setting powder.

STEP 5: FOUNDATION POWDER

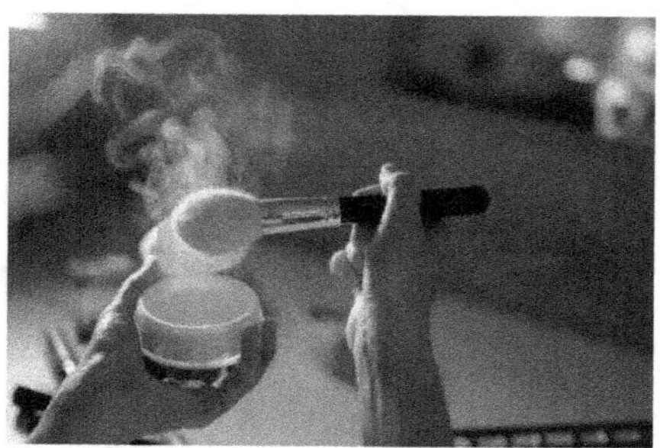

Applying foundation powder can be a tricky process; too little and you may as well have skipped the step altogether, too much and you'll be sporting the dreaded "cake look". In your quest for a flawless complexion, you've likely heard plenty of tricks of the trade regarding powder foundation. Keep these tips in mind to get that perfect complexion.

Using a large, fluffy powder brush, begin by dusting a light coat of powder all over your face. Press the bristles into the powder, then sweep across the skin in long, arching strokes.

If there are certain areas of your skin that need more coverage (the red and oily parts of your face are generally found in the center), you may want to apply a bit more powder. For this step, place your brush into the powder then firmly press it into the skin; this step helps the powder make its way into pores and lines for a smoother texture.

STEP 6: BRONZER

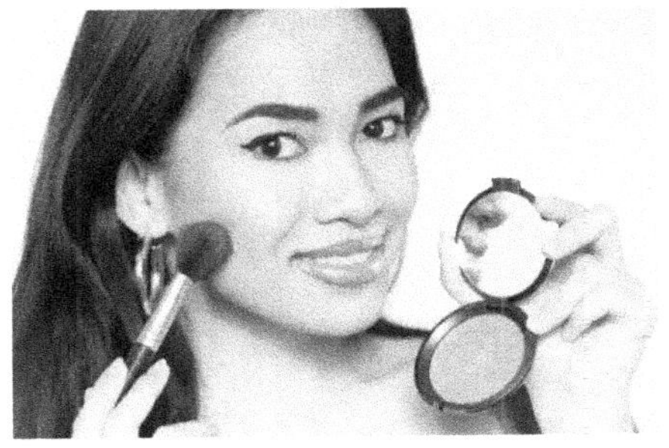

Bronzer can give your skin that sun-kissed glow all year long. Use a dedicated bronzer brush to sweep a golden tan across your face; bronzer brushes are crafted with more bristles, and placed much more tightly together, ensuring you get the most out of your colorful bronzer with each and every swipe

How to Choose the Right Shade of Bronzer

One of the most common bronzer blunders comes in choosing the wrong shade. If you're not used to working with bronzer, use one that's two shades darker than your skin at most.

Where to Apply Bronzer

Once you've got the right shade, apply your bronzer in the shape of a number "3" on both sides of the face. Start at your forehead, pull the bronzer along your cheeks, then sweep it across the jawline, reaching all the way down to your chin.

Pro Tip: Don't forget to blend it into your neck. Repeat on the opposite side.

STEP 7: BLUSH

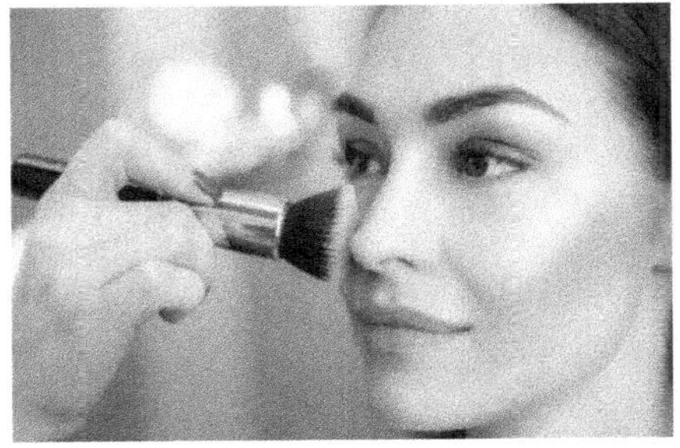

Flushed cheeks have been a mainstay of makeup glamor for centuries. If you want to add a bit more color and vibrancy to your complexion, blush may be the key. Use a dense brush with plenty of bristles to apply your blush—this will make sure you get the most out of every blush sweep.

Where to Apply Blush

There's not a one-size-fits-all answer for blush application. Use the color of your blush to help you decide where to apply it.

Pink blush: When using pink blush, apply it only to the apples of your cheeks. Pink blush is designed to mimic the natural flush your body creates, during which blood pools into your cheeks. To find the apples of your cheeks, put on your best smile. The "apple" refers to the front part of the cheek that becomes more pronounced when you sport a grin.

- **Plum blush:** Those with medium to dark skin tones can use plum blushes in the same way those with fair complexions use light pink blushes.
- **Peach blush:** Instead of using pink blush on just the apples of the cheeks, utilize these shades to help sculpt your face and add just a tiny hint of color. Twist one side

of your face (as if you were pursing your lips and directing them to the opposite side of the face). Then, sweep the peach blush along your cheekbones, starting near your ears and ending at the apples of your cheeks.

STEP 8: HIGHLIGHTER

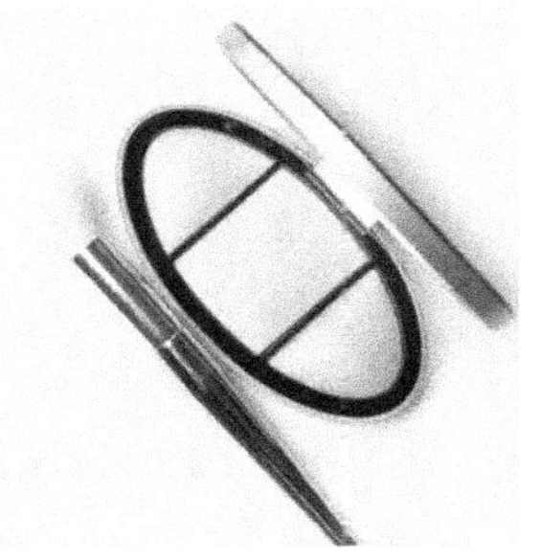

The right highlighter adds a bit of glam and glow to every makeup look. Whether you're opting for a more natural look or want something bold and beautiful, highlighter can complement your makeup application. Highlighters come in a variety of forms, including liquids, creams, and powders. You can choose to use one, or find your favorite combination of two or three. Whatever you choose, the application process remains the same.

Where to Apply Highlighter

After you've created a flawless canvas with your new foundation routine, map out the areas on your face that you wish to highlight.

Using a liquid highlighter first, apply in the following areas:

- Down the bridge of your nose.
- Across the tops of your cheekbones.
- In the inner corners of your eyelids.
- On your brow bone.
- The indent above your upper lip (also called the Cupid's Bow).
- The center of your forehead.
- The center of your chin.

Once you're happy with your liquid highlighter application, blend it in using your fingertips or a sponge. To maximize the effect of your highlighting, layer in cream or powder highlighter over the areas you wish to accentuate.

STEP 9: EYESHADOW

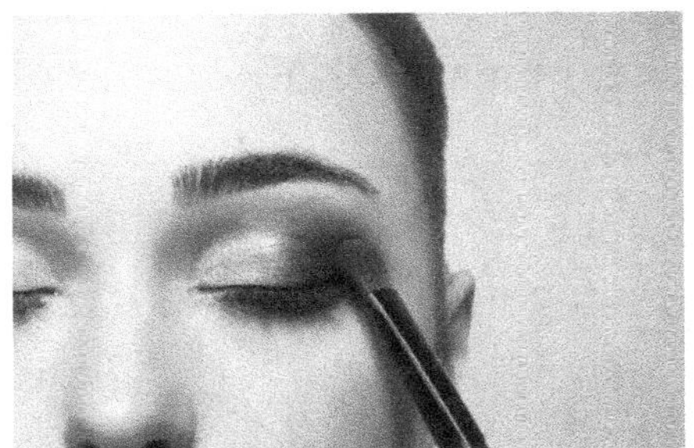

Eyeshadow can add interest to your makeup look, whether you opt for neutral shades or go bold with colorful hues. Whichever look you use, grab two complementary eyeshadows: one **lighter shade,** and one **darker shade**. Dip your eyeshadow brush into the light shade, then tap the brush to get rid of any excess product.

Application of Eyeshadow

Apply the lighter shadow across the entire lid, starting at the lash line and ending just above the crease of your eyelid. Now dip your brush into the darker color, tapping off the excess once again. Apply the color at the outer corner of your eye, just above your lash line. Sweep the darker color across your eyelid crease, just under the brow bone. Stop application around the center of your eyelid, as you don't want to darken the inner corners. Take a clean shadow brush and blend the two shades together. If you'd like a more intense look, reapply the darker shadow once more.

STEP 10: EYELINER

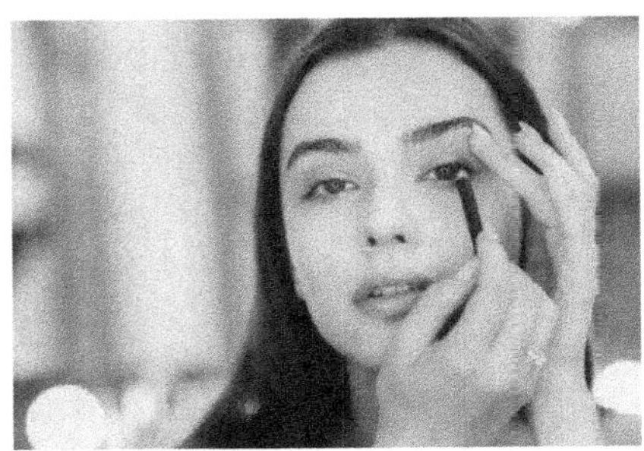

Applying eyeliner can be difficult—one little mistake and you're stuck with "raccoon" eyes. Banish your eye makeup woes with these essential tips for applying eyeliner.

Types of Eyeliner

1. **Liquid eyeliner:** If you're looking for precision, liquid eyeliner is your new best friend. You can find liquid liner in bottle form, which is applied with a fine dipping brush. You can also find liquid liner in a marker-type pen.

How to Apply Eyeliner

With liquid eyeliner, start thin at the inner corner of your eye, then make the application thicker towards the outer corner. You can start lining at the middle of your eye, or in the inner corner, and keep the liner tip or brush as close to the lash line as possible. Use small strokes of your liner to create small dashes along the lash line, then connect them to fill in the gaps. If your hand slips, don't worry! Apply a bit of eye makeup remover to a Q-tip and clean up the area.

2. **Gel eyeliner:** This type of eyeliner typically comes in a small pot, with a thin brush for application. Gel eyeliner is fantastic for creating a cat-eye look.

How to Apply Gel Eyeliner

Dip a flat, angular brush into the gel eyeliner pot. Swirl the brush to ensure both sides have product on them, and start application in the middle of the lash line, working outwards. Then, draw a line from the inner corner of your eye towards the middle, connecting the two lines.

3. **Pencil eyeliner:** This is typically the best eyeliner option for beginners. A sharp pencil eyeliner is easy to use on your waterline, and is great for creating a smokey eye.

How to Apply Pencil Eyeliner

Sharpen your liner pencil each time you use it. After pulling your eyelid taut, draw small light dots starting at the outer corner of your upper eyelid. Work your way into the inner corner of your eye to create a thin dotted line, as close to the lash line as possible. Connect the dots with your pencil or use a small shadow brush to blend them in.

STEP 11: MASCARA

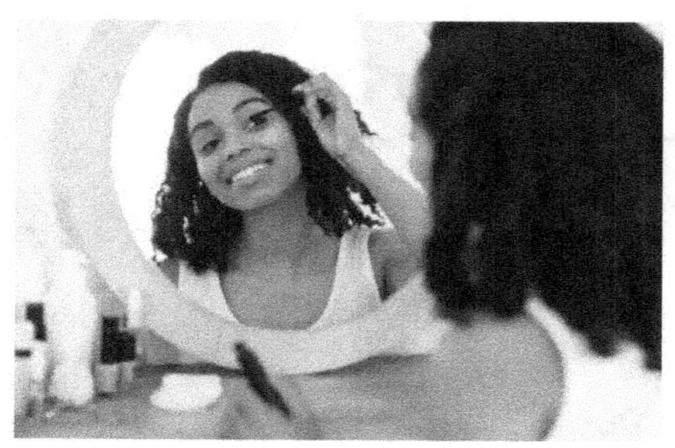

If you're going to use only one makeup product, mascara should be at the top of your list. A few swipes of mascara can make your eyes look brighter in a single step. You can find mascara in a variety of colors, but black and brown tend to be the most popular. Start by curling your eyelashes with an eyelash curler.

How to curl your eyelashes:

- Place the curler at the base of your upper lashes, being careful not to grab any of the sensitive skin around your eyelid.
- Slowly close the curler.
- Hold it in place for a few seconds.
- Release gently.

After your eyelashes are curled, grab your tube of mascara. Gently swirl the wand around to ensure all the bristles are coated in mascara. Pro Tip: Don't pump the wand into the tube, as this allows air to get in and may cause your mascara to clump. Wriggle the mascara brush lightly across the roots of your lashes. This will create more volume, which you can then pull through to the ends of your lashes. If your lashes clump together, grab a clean wand and brush through them. Apply a second coat for more volume.

STEP 12: LIP GLOSS

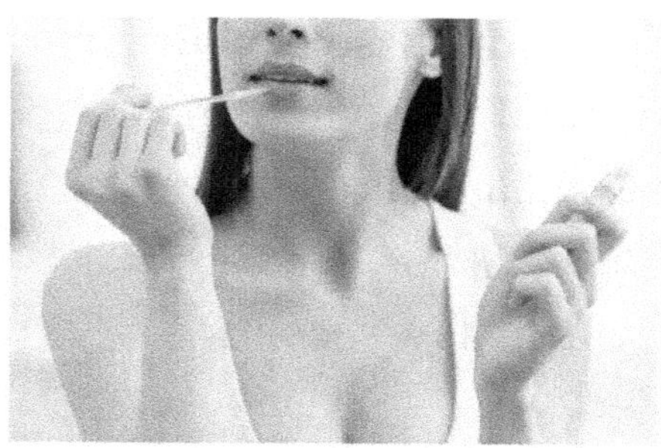

Before applying gloss, prep your lips. If your lips are chapped and cracked, be sure to use a gentle lip scrub to remove any dead skin and apply a protective lip gloss.

How to Apply Lip Gloss

Use a lip conditioner or moisturizer to soften the lips further. After your lip balm has absorbed, blot any excess. Begin applying your lip gloss from the center of your lips, and drag the applicator along the length of your pout. Try to avoid pulling any gloss above your natural lip line, and smack your lips together lightly to ensure your lip gloss reaches all the nooks and crannies of your lips.

STEP 13: SETTING SPRAY & SETTING POWDER

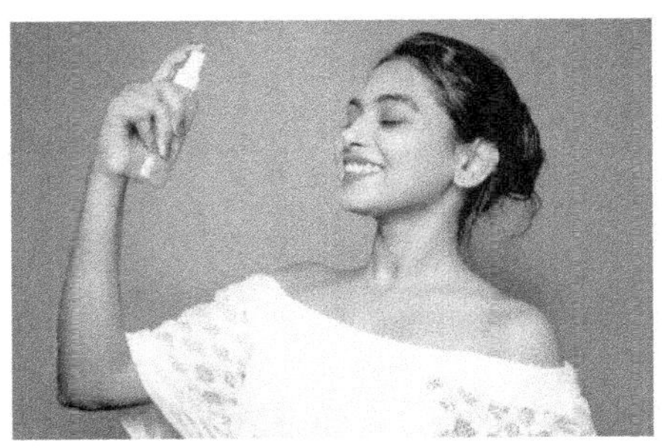

Setting spray or setting powder can be the final touch for your makeup routine. If you want makeup that stays on all day long, without greasing, creasing, or shine, it's important to invest in a quality setting solution. Setting sprays are designed for all skin types, and can be used to set a variety of looks, whether you're rocking light coverage or sporting a full face of beautiful makeup. Setting spray keeps your makeup in place, helping you reduce reapplication needs and keeping your makeup looking flawless for hours at a time. Setting spray is to your face as hairspray is to your stylish do, and it's applied in a very similar fashion. Hold the bottle at least 8 inches from your face, then spritz lightly a few times to ensure all bits of your face are covered. If you want to ensure your makeup is covered from forehead to chin, first spritz in an X shape across your face, then follow it up by spraying a T shape.

There's no need to rub the spray in once applied, as it will dry naturally within seconds.

FINAL LOOK

Your makeup is complete. With these makeup application tips, it's easy to create a variety of beauty looks, whether you're headed to the office or going out for a night on the town.

The Secrets of Beauty

CHAPTER 4

BUILDING YOUR BEAUTY ROUTINE

Great skin is not simply a matter of DNA — your daily habits, in fact, have a big impact on what you see in the mirror. But depending on which product reviews you read or doctors you consult, there is a dizzying number of opinions on everything from how to moisturize to how to protect yourself from UV rays. Ultimately, caring for your skin is simply personal. It's not enough to have good skin-care products: For your products to be most effective, you also need to apply them in the correct order. Your routine will depend on your skin type, the ingredients and formulations of your products, and the time of day.

Know Your Skin Type

The right routine starts with knowing what kind of skin you have. Then you'll know how to take care of it. Once you've determined your skin type, you can narrow down which products to look for, and which ones to avoid. Many products will indicate on their label what sort of skin type they're best for, making it easy to find products that'll work for you.

I. Dry skin is flaky, scaly, or rough.
II. Oily skin is shiny, greasy, and may have big pores.
III. Combination skin is dry in some spots (cheeks) and oily in others (forehead, nose, and chin).
IV. Sensitive skin may sting, burn, or itch after you use some makeup or other products.

V.   Normal skin is balanced, clear, and not sensitive.

CHOOSE A CLEANSER

A cleanser removes the dirt, oil, and bacteria that you come in contact with during the day, or at night while you sleep. This first step in your routine is critical. Cleansing your face will help you start or end your day with fresh skin. Additionally, you'll be able to receive the maximum benefits from the products you apply after cleansing, because your face will be free of any dirt and debris that would impact the way products are absorbed.

Patients with oily skin should look for foaming cleansers that remove excess oil and pore-clogging bacteria, while patients with dry skin should look for hydrating cleansers to help restore the skin's moisture barrier.

A dermatologist, will recommend effective cleansers such as:

The Secrets of Beauty

I.   Epionce Lytic Gel Cleanser: For all skin types

II.   Cerave Hydrating Facial Cleanser: For dry skin types

III.   Cetaphil Gentle Skin Cleanser: For sensitive skin types

Cleaning Normal/Combo Skin

Don't just grab whatever soap is in the shower or at the sink to wash your face. And don't feel like you have to buy fancy, expensive products, either. Just find skin care that works for you. Apply a gentle cleanser or soap with your fingertips. Don't scrub your face. Rinse with plenty of warm water, then pat dry. If your skin dries out or gets oily, try a different cleanser.

Cleaning Dry Skin

For this skin type, use a gentle cleanser that doesn't have alcohol or fragrances. Those ingredients can dry you out even more. Gently wash your skin, then rinse with plenty of warm water. Don't use hot water -- it removes the natural oils from your face faster. Try exfoliating once a week to get rid of flaky skin cells. It will make your skin look clearer and more even.

Cleaning Oily Skin

Use an oil-free foaming cleanser to wash your face. Rinse with plenty of warm water. You may want to use a toner or astringent after, but be careful because it might irritate your skin. These products can remove extra oil, which makes your face less shiny, and help keep skin clean.

Cleaning Sensitive Skin

Wash your face with a gentle cleanser and rinse with warm water. Don't rub your skin with a towel -- gently pat it dry. Exfoliating may irritate sensitive skin. Try not to use products that have alcohol, soap, acid, or fragrance. Instead, look on the label for calming ingredients like aloe, chamomile, green tea polyphenols, and oats. The fewer ingredients in a product, the happier your face may be.

FIND THE RIGHT MOISTURIZER

You may think you're too young to need moisturizer -- or your skin is too oily -- but all skin types need one every day. Apply it while your skin is still damp from washing or rinsing to help seal in moisture. If you have acne or your skin is oily, find a moisturizer that's lightweight and oil-free, so it won't block your pores. Your skin needs moisture to replenish the water it loses throughout the day. Moisturizers with ingredients such as ceramides and hyaluronic acid can provide your skin with the healthy hydration it needs to stay soft, supple, and youthful. Even if you have oily or combination skin, it's still important to moisturize. In fact, a lack of moisture can drive your skin to produce more oil in order to compensate for it, which can lead to clogged pores and breakouts.

To give your skin the moisture it needs, we recommend the following moisturizers:

I. **Vanicream Moisturizing Skin Cream:** For all skin types
II. **Eucerin Moisturizing Face Lotion:** For all skin types
III. **Neutrogena Hydro Boost Water Gel :** For oily skin types

Put on Sunscreen

Your moisturizer may already have sunscreen in it. But it's a good idea to use separate protection, too. The sun can damage your skin in only 15 minutes. Look for a sunscreen that gives broad-spectrum protection with an SPF of at least 30. Wear it every day, even if it's not sunny and even if it's cold. Reapply every 2 hours. We find that many patients only use sunscreen during what seems like the obvious times to do so, like a sunny day at the beach. But, in reality, it's important to wear sunscreen every day. In addition to reducing your skin cancer risk, you'll also be preventing the effects of photoaging—which can include dark spots and wrinkles.

Many moisturizers and cosmetics contain SPF, making it easy for you to get the sun protection you need without buying more than one product. Whether you get your protection from cosmetic products or from stand-alone sunscreens, make sure the formula contains broad-spectrum SPF 30 or higher to ensure you're as protected as possible.

There are many sunscreens on the market that can provide safe sun protection. Some of our favorites include:

I. **La Roche-Posay Ultra-Light Sunscreen:** For sensitive or dry skin types
II. **Eucerin Sun Lotion:** For all skin types

III.   **Blue Lizard Sensitive Sunscreen:** For sensitive skin types

WHEN SHOULD YOU WASH?

You can dry your skin by washing it too much, so once a day is fine for most people. In the morning, rinse your face with lukewarm water. Use a soft towel to pat it dry. At night, washing with a cleanser or gentle soap gets rid of the day's dirt and makeup. If you exercise, play sports, or have PE, you may want to wash your face afterward with a gentle cleanser. Sweat can clog your pores and make acne worse.

Don't Wear Makeup to Bed

When you're tired, it can be tempting to go to bed without washing your face. But leaving makeup on your skin can clog your pores and cause acne. So wash it off with a gentle cleanser or makeup remover. Use a soft wash cloth or cotton pads. If you use acne medicine, now's a good time to put it on when your face is clean and you won't be putting on makeup.

All About Acne

Why does acne usually start when you're a teen? Puberty causes your body to make more hormones, which lead your skin to make more sebum, an oil that comes from your pores. Too much sebum and dead skin cells can clog pores and trap bacteria inside. The germs thrive and acne starts. It can show up as whiteheads, blackheads, and pimples.

How to Treat Acne

Don't pop those pimples! That can lead to infection and scars. Instead, try acne-fighting products. They come as lotions, creams, gels, and cleansing pads. Follow the directions carefully. If you use them too much or too often, they can irritate your skin and cause more blemishes. Just be patient -- they can take 8 weeks to work. If your acne is really bad, get help from a dermatologist.

Topical acne treatments containing ingredients such as benzoyl peroxide and salicylic acid can reduce the number of breakouts you experience, as well as help acne heal faster. These treatments should be applied immediately after you cleanse your skin. When applying these treatments, remember to plan ahead. Most acne treatments need at least 5-15 minutes to dry before you can proceed with the rest of your routine

Hiding Blemishes

To make zits less noticeable, you can cover them with oil-free makeup. Foundation may help cover large patches of acne. Concealer covers smaller areas. Green-tinted color-correcting concealers may cancel out redness. You also can hide acne and treat it at the same time. Some tinted creams and concealers contain salicylic acid or benzoyl peroxide to help dry the blemishes. Stop using any product if it bothers your skin or causes more acne.

The Dangers of Tanning

You may like to be tan, but you hurt your skin when it changes color from the sun or indoor tanning. UV exposure can make you more likely to get skin cancer -- now or later. It can also lead to wrinkly, leathery-looking skin and spots. Regularly using tanning beds raises your chances of getting melanoma (the deadliest skin cancer) by 8 times.

Fake Tans

For a safer tan, try sunless self-tanner. It stains your skin and comes in many forms, including lotions, sprays, and towelettes. Or try airbrush tanning, where a salon expert sprays the tan right on your skin. For a quick fake tan, try some bronzer. It's a brush-on powder or tinted cream that gives the look of a fresh tan. But remember you'll still need to protect your skin from the sun.

Choosing Makeup

If you wear makeup, choose products that have "non acnegenic" or "non comedogenic" on the label. They should be less likely to cause acne or clog pores. Look for makeup that's water-based and not oil-based. Some products have expiration dates, even though they aren't required. Most of the time, you'll need to replace eye makeup first. For example, don't use mascara longer than 4 months.

Makeup Safety Tips

Don't share makeup or makeup tools. Use fresh applicators when you try on makeup in stores. Don't apply eyeliner inside your lid, because it may irritate your eye. If you've had an eye infection, buy new makeup so you don't reinfect yourself. Never put on makeup in a car or on the bus. A bump or swerve could make you scratch your eye or get makeup and germs in it.

False Advertising

Seeing a model's perfect skin in an ad may make you want to buy the product. Don't be fooled. It takes a team of stylists and professionals to get them to look that great. Graphic artists can digitally remove pimples and freckles. Lighting experts use light and shadow to show the model's best features. CVS drugstores have pledged to move toward non-retouched photos in store displays.

Other Things That Bug Your Skin

I.   Try to avoid habits that can cause acne, redness, and scars.

II. Don't pick at your skin, especially pimples. Keep hairspray and gel away from your face. They can clog pores.

III. Don't wear tight headbands or wool hats that can irritate your skin.

IV.   Don't smoke. It can age your skin and make it yellow and dry.

Food and Sleep for Healthy Skin

Keep your skin healthy by eating smart. Fill your plate with veggies, fruits, and whole grains. Choose lean proteins like chicken, fish, lean meat, beans, and eggs. Avoid foods that are high in cholesterol, trans fats, saturated fats, salt, and sugar. Get plenty of sleep to avoid dark circles, fine lines, dull skin, and other side effects of bad rest. Relax! Even stress can make you break out. And stay hydrated.

The Secrets of Beauty

CHAPTER 5

NATURAL BEAUTY PRODUCTS

Do you also feel that natural ingredients are more skin-friendly than artificial ingredients? Most of us have strong faith in natural ingredients over chemical products when it comes to skincare. And it is justified as well. Consumers are well aware of the harmful effects of chemicals, and many choose products that promise to be all-natural. In this article, we bring you all the know-how about natural ingredients that are scientifically proven to deliver benefits for your skin.

How To Find Real Natural Ingredients?

When you choose a skincare product, you look for ingredients that have zero side effects on your skin. You look for a product that is all-natural and perfectly suits your skin type. This quest for a natural product would lead to checking the listing of the natural ingredients in it.

The natural compound can either be applied topically or consumed orally through your meals. While this can be done through over-the-counter products, homemade solutions are available too. These homemade methods can help you obtain the benefits from the natural elements. The most common natural items people use for skin care includes aloe vera, tea tree oil, bentonite clay, argan oil etc. Whether consumed orally or applied topically, it is however important to consider that the real natural ingredient suits your skin type and addresses your skin concerns.

What Are The Safe Natural Ingredients For Skin?

The Secrets of Beauty

1. Aloe Vera

Aloe vera plant has many healing properties and is proven to be effective in treating several skin conditions. Naturally, its benefits make it the most popular topical gel among people.

How Does It Help?

I.   Aloe vera is extremely useful in treating cuts, wounds and burns. The gel gives a soothing relief from the stinging sensation caused by wounds or burns.

II.   It works as a natural healer for your skin.

III.   Applying aloe vera gel prevents scar formation and fights against bacterial infections.

IV.   It has the potential of dealing with severe skin conditions like eczema, psoriasis and cold sores.

V.   Reducing dark circles, protecting against sunburn, acting as an anti-ageing agent are various other roles of aloe-vera.

The Secrets of Beauty

2. Bentonite Clay

Bentonite clay is a natural clay that is known for its absorption quality. It has been used in medical science and for skincare purposes since ages.

How Does It Help?

I. Bentonite absorbs all the toxins from your skin, making skin clean and healthy.

II. It also removes the excessive oil, bacteria and dirt from your skin.

III. Since it absorbs the excess sebum oil, the oil balance of your skin gets better, which leads to lesser acne.

IV. It is also proven to be effective on poison ivy rashes. A report made in 1995 clearly states that bentonite is potent for curing poison ivy allergies.

V. You can also use it on your baby to reduce diaper rashes. Studies suggest that bentonite clay improves diaper rashes within just a few hours.

3. Hyaluronic Acid

Hyaluronic acid is naturally found in the human body and acts as a humectant. It helps to lock the moisture into your skin and keep it hydrated all the time. Natural sources of hyaluronic acid are potatoes, soy-based foods, red wine, avocado, almonds, green vegetables etc.

How Does It Help?

I. Topical application of hyaluronic acid improves the condition of dry skin as well as fight against anti-ageing signs such as fine lines, wrinkles, age spots etc.

II. It is also a source of antioxidants for your skin.

III. Hyaluronic acid has anti-inflammation and healing properties that help wounds to heal faster.

IV. With age, the body starts lacking hyaluronic acid, leading to wrinkles and fine lines. Then you need to replenish hyaluronic acid either topically or through your regular diet.

4. Lauric Acid

Lauric acid is one of the most common natural ingredients that's used everyday. It is a saturated fat that is majorly found in coconut oil. You must be aware of the worldwide usage of coconut oil for skin and hair care products. Milk and palm also have a fair share of lauric acid. It can also be found in the human body in a solid and insoluble form.

How Does It Help?

I.   Lauric acid works for acne treatment as well as an anti-ageing element.
II.   It can also help battle against skin diseases like psoriasis and xerosis cutis.
III. The moisturization ability of lauric acid prevents dry skin and makes skin supple.

5. Kojic Acid

Kojic acid is a natural metabolite derived from fungi named Aspergillus. You may have noticed most face serums and depigmentation creams contain Kojic acid. You can also find soaps and cleansers that have Kojic acid in them.

How Does It Help?

I.   Kojic acid is considered to be antibacterial and antifungal in nature. Thus, it works against yeast infection, ringworm and candidiasis.

II.   It is used as a skin lightening element in treating depigmentation or similar skin conditions like melasma.

III.   It can also protect you from sun damage.

6. Tea Tree Oil

Tea tree oil has a history in skincare for hundreds of years.

How Does It Help?

I.   It has been used to treat acne breakouts, reduce inflammation and redness on the skin.

II.   It has antimicrobial, anti-fungal and anti-inflammatory properties.

III.   When applied directly to your skin, it serves a lot of purposes that include skin moisturization, scar treatment, protection against skin infection etc.

IV.   It also works well for skin conditions like eczema and psoriasis.

7. Grape Seed Oil

Grapeseed oil is a natural compound that is used in many skincare products. As the name suggests, the oil is extracted from grape seeds. It contains antioxidants and linoleic acid that offers a lot for your skin.

How Does It Help?

I. While antioxidants keep your skin hydrated and fight against free radicals, linoleic acid reduces acne.

II. It is considered to be a non-comedogenic element, which makes it suitable for sensitive skin as well.

III. Grape seed oil has anti-inflammatory properties that work in favor of acne-prone skin.

8. Argan Oil

Argan oil is a plant-derived ingredient. It is extracted from kernels that grow in argan trees. It is used worldwide both orally and topically to obtain skin benefits. It is enriched with beneficial properties and essential vitamins.

How Does It Help?

I. Sun protection, acne treatment, and skin moisturization are common traits of argan oil.

II. It also deals with several skin conditions like psoriasis, rosacea and atopic dermatitis.

9. Coffee Beans

Coffee is a massive source of antioxidants which is beneficial for your skin in many ways.

How Does It Help?

I. It hydrates your skin and reduces aging signs like fine lines, age spots and wrinkles. In short, it can be an anti-ageing element for your skin.

II. Coffee scrub is an excellent way to get even-toned and smooth skin.

III. It has anti-inflammatory properties which can help reduce acne.

IV. It also works on dark circles. Topical usage of caffeine under the eyes is a popular method of reducing dark circles.

10. Phytosphingosine

Phytosphingosine is a fatty lipid found in animals, plants and a few fungi. It is known for its water-attracting and water-repelling properties. Many known brands use Phytosphingosine in their skincare products. It is mostly recommended for people with dry and flaky skin.

The Secrets of Beauty

How Does It Help?

I. The most important role of Phytosphingosine is protecting the skin barrier.

II. It works as a shield and stops irritants and pollutants from harming your skin barrier.

III. Phytosphingosine locks the moisture in your skin to keep it hydrated. This is how it maintains the natural moisturizing factor (NMF) of your skin.

Natural ingredients are indeed better than most chemical compounds used in skincare products. But not all-natural ingredients are free from side effects. Some of them may have mild side effects on your skin as well. So, it is always better to conduct a patch test before using any product. Also, you need to know your skin and choose ingredients that would help you out with your specific skin concerns.

The Secrets of Beauty

CHAPTER 6

DIY BEAUTY RECIPES

Cosmetics and beauty products are a major source of chemical exposure for most people. An average beauty product contains dozens of harmful chemicals, many of which have not even been tested for safety in humans!

Fortunately, there are natural alternatives for every beauty product, and most work better than the chemical-laden alternatives. I have made hundreds of natural beauty and personal care recipes over the years — from shampoo and conditioner to mascara and foundation! I know it might seem like you need a cabinet of special ingredients, but you can make so many great recipes with what's in your kitchen plus just a few key bulk purchases!

Here's how to get started:

INGREDIENTS FOR NATURAL BEAUTY RECIPES

These seven products are my natural beauty staples… (There's a list of recipes I use below!) If you're just starting out with DIY beauty products, these are great to have on hand and you can make many, many recipes with just these ingredients!

1. Coconut Oil

The Secrets of Beauty

I ordered Gold Label Coconut Oil in five gallon buckets from Tropical Traditions. This is by far my favorite coconut oil and I can tell a difference in taste and quality. We save a lot by buying in bulk, and since we use it to cook, in recipes and as a skin lotion by itself, it never goes to waste! (It also comes in smaller quantities!) We will only use Unrefined, organic coconut oil in cooking, but a cheaper expeller pressed oil could be used in skin recipes to save money (though by ordering in bulk, we still get the good stuff for cheaper than the expeller pressed in the long run!).

For those sensitive to coconut, grass fed organic beef tallow can also be used and it is great for the skin, though you will need to add essential oils to cover the mild scent. We get our tallow in five gallon buckets here.

2. Shea Butter

Our most used natural beauty ingredient after coconut oil. Organic unrefined shea butter has a naturally nutty, earthy smell (very mild) and is incredibly nourishing for the skin! I've heard many cases of children seeing improvement from eczema from using shea butter or a mix of it and coconut oil.

It has natural antibacterial properties and is great for preventing stretch marks, for wound healing, and as an anti-aging treatment for skin. It naturally has an SPF of about 5 and can be used as a daily sunscreen. I use shea butter in my lotion, lotion bars, deodorant, face cream, baby lotion, diaper cream and many other recipes!

3. Cocoa Butter

Cocoa butter is another "butter" and a great addition to natural beauty recipes. It is also an ingredient in organic homemade chocolate (recipe soon!). It imparts a delicate chocolate scent, and I love it mixed with mint or citrus in lotion bars, lotion or face cream. It can be used interchangeably with Shea Butter, though I find that my favorite recipes include Shea butter, Cocoa Butter, and Coconut Oil.

4. Beeswax

Beeswax is a great natural thickening agent, and high quality versions have a gentle honey scent. (Note: I've heard from several readers that brands ordered from other sources had a very strong and off-putting odor and I can only vouch for this brand.) I use beeswax in lotions, lotion bars, baby care recipes, lip balm, foot cream, etc. Only a little is usually needed to thicken recipes, and a pound lasts us for at least six months.

5. Liquid Carrier Oil

Recipes like smoother lotions, baby oil, salves, and after-shave balms often need to be thinner than coconut oil and the butters will allow. In these cases, I use a liquid carrier oil. Most often, I use olive oil, almond oil, or apricot kernel oil (my favorite). Apricot Kernel has the most gentle scent and almond oil is also relatively unscented. Olive oil is typically the least expensive if you don't mind the olive scent in your recipes or if you plan to cover it up with essential oils.

6. Arrowroot Powder

I keep Arrowroot on hand for thickening sauces when cooking and it also gets added to a lot of natural recipes like deodorant, baby powder, diaper cream, dry shampoo, etc. It works much like cornstarch but isn't GMO like many corn products. I also use it in my homemade makeup recipes. I've only used this brand, and others have reported that brands from elsewhere are often not as finely ground and don't work as well in skin recipes.

7. Essential Oils

Not technically needed, but essential oils give great natural scents to DIY beauty recipes and can also be very mood lifting. I get mine here in 8 ounce or larger quantities and they last literally years. Our favorites are mint, lavender, lemon, orange, and sandalwood.

Other Helpful Ingredients

Some other helpful ingredients that can be added to the above recipes are:

- **Dried herbs:** especially chamomile and calendula for skin recipes
- **Zinc oxide:** for diaper cream and sunscreens
- **Sugar:** Not to eat but great for sugar scrubs!
- **Baking soda:** For deodorant
- **Salt:** For DIY hair spray or skin exfoliating

Other essential oils

- **Coconut milk:** for homemade shampoo

- **Liquid castile soap:** for cleaning/washing and for homemade baby wipes.

CHAPTER 7

BEAUTY ON A BUDGET

When it comes to beauty, there are so many things that we think we need to improve. We want our lashes lifted, our nails manicured, and our legs lasered! And it's not easy on our budgets.

I recently saw a study commissioned by Groupon on beauty spending habits. According to the survey, women who invest in their appearance spend an average of $3,756 every year on beauty.

Here are 10 beauty secrets that will keep your budget happy.

1. Haircuts and Manicures

Women know a good haircut can cost upwards of $50. Add some color, and suddenly you're into the hundreds!

But here's the secret to getting a great cut for significantly less:

Book an appointment at your local cosmetology school. These students are up on the latest hair trends, but they also need practice. If you're nervous about a first-day student butchering your locks, ask for a more experienced stylist—and make sure he or she is being supervised. While you're at it, check out their prices on manicures, pedicures and eyebrow shaping. Or buy a gel set and do it yourself at home.

2. Shampoos and Conditioners

2 Ways To Save Money On Quality Shampoo and Conditioner

There are two main ways to save money on quality shampoo and conditioner.

1. **The first is to shop at off-price stores** like Ross, T.J.Maxx and Marshalls. The only downside is that the selection

constantly changes. So, buy what you can when you see your favorite products, because they might not be there the next time—just don't blow your budget on impulse. For example, if you go ahead and buy it when you see it in the store, just be sure to adjust your budget so you can keep hitting your financial goals.

II. **The second way is to buy store-brand or generic versions of the designer product.** For example, I have it on very good authority that Kirkland Signature Professional Salon Formula Moisture Shampoo and Conditioner at Costco are made by Pureology. Switching to Costco's version will put $50 per bottle back in your budget.

3. Hairspray and Texture Spray

Don't assume that just because it's at the drugstore or grocery store means it's no good. In fact, many times, my local Kroger surprises me with the high-end brands they carry. But if you're getting out of debt or building an emergency fund, beauty on a budget means trying less expensive brands. And don't forget to check Amazon when you're comparing prices. My favorite hair product of all time is L'Oréal Paris Advanced Boost It Spray (I use it on my roots), and it's less than $4 on Amazon.

4. Fashionable Eyewear

As someone who kept tiny, round, out-of-style eyeglasses for decades, I understand how hard it is to bite the bullet and spend money on new glasses. But these days, it's so easy to update your look with online companies like Warby Parker. Start budgeting with EveryDollar today!

With Warby Parker, all you have to do is choose five different frames to try from their website. They'll ship your choices right to your door so you can try them on in the comfort of your own home. Once you know which ones you want, you return the frames, submit your prescription, and get a cute new pair of glasses for cheap! The best part is that these companies believe eyewear should be affordable. Getting your glasses through one of them will keep your bill under $100.

5. Statement Earrings

Everyone loves the big, bold statement earrings these days—including me. They can make any outfit more fun! Which leads me to one of my favorite fashion hacks of the last decade. Are you ready? Get your statement earrings on Amazon. They come in every color and style imaginable, and they're so dang cheap—like this 20-pack for $22. Yes, for real. I wear these on The Rachel Cruze Show all the time, and I love them! I have the money tendency of quantity over quality, so this makes my heart sing.

6. Skin Care

The Secrets of Beauty

Regardless of what some infomercial or your dermatologist sold you on years ago, you don't need to spend an arm and a leg on a good skin care routine. A 2019 investigation researched the real differences between high-end moisturizers and the ones you can buy at a drugstore. They found that both expensive and affordable moisturizers use the same ingredients.

Dr. Rachel Nazarian reported, "Hyaluronic acid is hyaluronic acid. A brand like Neutrogena will make a phenomenal one that, to me, is just as good as these fancy ones that you'll pay $100, $200 for." If you're spending hundreds on skin care, this is a great area to put money back in your budget. Personally, I swear by CeraVe facial moisturizer. It's cheap, it has SPF coverage, and you can get it at any drugstore.

7. Massages and Facials

You don't have to wait for Mother's Day or Valentine's Day to hit the spa. If you have a massage school in town, you can snag a quick shiatsu for $20–30. Or check with your local cosmetology school for deals on a professional-quality facial. One of my favorite skin care techniques is called **dermaplaning**. It involves scraping the top layer of dead skin off of your face with a small razor. It sounds crazy, but it will leave your skin feeling the smoothest it's ever been! Watch a couple tutorials on YouTube, order the tool from Amazon for cheap, and you're good to go. Trust me, if I can do it at home, you can too!

8. Makeup Brushes

When it comes to beauty items that bust the budget, I know people love high-quality makeup brushes. I have a really nice one for applying foundation. But for the basics like eyeshadow and blush, the affordable drugstore brushes work just as well, and they last forever. And you can wash the brush every so often with soap and warm water.

9. Workout Plans

If you need the motivation of going to an actual gym, there are several chains like Workout Anytime that start around $10/month. Your local YMCA will also have a sliding scale where your monthly fee is based on your income.

10. Frequency

One of the best ways to maintain beauty on a budget is to simply cut back. If you want to make your money go further, you'll need to reconsider weekly manicures or monthly false eyelashes. If you wash your hair every other day instead of daily, your shampoo and conditioner will last twice as long. And what if you went minimalist with your makeup? How much time and money would that save you?

Picture yourself 20 or 30 years from now, living in retirement. Will touching up your highlights twice a year instead of once every six weeks have a major impact on what you're doing? It might, if you invested that money instead.

What if you could save $3,000 on beauty this year? How much faster would you be out of debt? How much sooner would you finish up your emergency fund?

When you're in control over your money, you feel confident in yourself. You're living out your values and creating a life you love. How beautiful is that?

The Secrets of Beauty

CHAPTER 8

COMMON BEAUTY MISTAKES TO AVOID

Some of us are often unaware of the makeup mistakes we commit every day. Finding the shades and brands of makeup that suit your face is a tricky task in the first place. It might take years for some to get their makeup right. And once you have found the right products, you might still struggle to create the desired look. Your favorite beauty influencer might make it look simple, but the truth is blending makeup to perfection is no easy task. But that does not mean you have to stop experimenting. We are here to explain the common makeup faux pas that you should avoid. This will help you figure out the dos and don'ts and ensure that your makeup is on fleek. Swipe up!

Most Common Makeup Mistakes And Beauty Blunders

1. Over-Washing Your Face

Cleansing or washing your face is the first and the most important step in makeup. Every woman has a different skin type, and with age, our skin undergoes many changes. But once you apply foundation and notice dry, flaky skin, it is a sign that you have to stop over-washing your face.

It is ideal to wash your face twice daily – once in the morning, and once at night, before you go to sleep. It is best to use a mild, gentle cleanser.

The natural skin oils work wonders on your skin and do their job without the interference of soap.

2. Applying Makeup On Dry Skin

Applying makeup on dry skin is one of the biggest makeup mistakes, which can make the face look dull, cracked, old, and tired. Everything good is built on a solid foundation, and in this case, a properly moisturized face. So, ensure that your face is properly hydrated before you apply makeup.

Haley Kim, a YouTuber, shares the mistakes that she made in her 20s and how she has recognized those mistakes and rectified them later. She admits, " I didn't even know about the importance of prepping my skin with good skincare before doing my makeup, so my skin looks cakey dry and matte, even though I had the most youthful skin in my 20s."

3. Makeup Application In The Wrong Lighting

When you need to decide what works for you and what doesn't with regard to makeup, you need to test it on your skin in natural lighting. When you try on makeup in unnatural lighting, you will notice that it doesn't look as flattering as you hoped. Pick what suits you best in the best lighting possible.

4. Wrong Blending Techniques

Makeup is much more than dabbing on a blush or eyeshadow. Even if you apply a neutral shade, it is going to look unnatural and out of place, unless you blend it properly. The key to natural looking makeup lies in mastering the art of blending. Makeup that isn't blended well can look quite comical. Watch some makeup videos and tutorials online and invest in a few good brushes to get started.

5. Incorrect Application Of Concealer

There's always a conflict when it comes to deciding whether the foundation goes first or the concealer. It does make more sense to cover the flaws once the foundation is set, which means it's better to use the foundation before the concealer. But when you do so, here are two things you must keep in mind.

I. **Never use too much product at once in the targeted area.** Too much concealer on your dark circles will make you look older. The correct way to cover dark circles is to dot a few drops of color-corrector concealer on the bone below your eyes and blend it up. Also, do not apply it directly to dark circles. You can also use the layering technique. Apply a little over a blemish, allow it to dry, and then apply another layer. You can also use a setting powder between the layers

II. **You can't use one concealer for everything.** Concealers are available in many colors, each having different uses. A peach-toned corrector concealer cancels out the blue and is best to combat dark circles. Green cancels out red, therefore a green-toned concealer must be used to hide pimples and blemishes. Yellow-toned concealers are best to even out large areas of your skin. Once you use these tinted concealers as the first layer, you need to follow it up with a concealer that matches your skin tone.

6. Too Much Foundation

Over- application of foundation will do no good to your face, and your makeup will end up looking cakey. Or worse, you look like a clown in costume. In fact, unless you are wearing light and sheer makeup, you don't need to use foundation all over the face. Simply apply it on your cheeks, nose, and under-eye areas. Some women use it to cover blemishes, and unevenness, but that is a concealer's job.

Ensure that you pick the right shade of foundation that matches perfectly with your skin tone. Don't use a foundation lighter than your skin tone. Using the wrong shade will only accentuate the blemishes, fine lines and all that is bad about your skin. Using a shade that matches your skin, is the only way you are going to get that flawless face. And never forget to blend properly. Make sure to apply it on your neck and ears as well. Otherwise, with a different face and neck color, everyone can figure out that you are wearing makeup

Quick Tip

For a natural look, apply foundation in the center of the face and blend outwards. This catches the target spots like cheekbones and corners of the mouth.

7. Eyebrow Disaster

Eyebrows frame those beautiful eyes that are, as they say, the windows to the soul. Neatly shaped eyebrows can highlight the eyes beautifully. Bushy eyebrows or overdrawn eyebrows look untidy and unkempt. Thin or tadpole-shaped eyebrows don't flatter your eyes either and will change your look entirely. It is essential to go to a professional and get proper advice on how your eyebrows must be shaped.

Over the years, it is normal for your eyebrows to diminish, and then you start filling them up. However, the last thing you want is for them to look drawn and unnatural. A brow pencil works best to give you that natural look. You must avoid harsh lines at all costs.

A dark shadow applied with an angled brush works better than a pencil. You can also use eyebrow cake powders that have everything you require for perfect brows in one little package.

8. Unwanted Shimmer And Glitter

Shimmery eyeshadows are very attractive, but when you use them over the entire eyelid, they can look extremely shiny and over the top. Use shimmery eyeshadow on the inner eye area, or in the center of the eyelid to make your eye makeup pop, and go for a matte shadow for the rest. Ideally, use nude eyeshadows, or eyeshadows that are a couple of shades darker than your skin tone.

9. Using The Wrong Eyeliner

It is advisable to use black eyeliner only if you have a darker skin tone, else it ends up looking quite harsh. If you have a lighter skin tone, it is best you stick to brown liners. Black is a no-no if you have blond hair and blue eyes.

Here are a few tips on how to use your eyeliner:

I.   Always pick a lighter or a more subtle color for your bottom lids.

II.   Using a liner on your waterline is not a good idea. Instead, use a nude pencil on your waterline as it will help open up your eyes, and make them look wider.

III. For a more natural look, it is best to apply it only to three-fourths of the upper eyelid.

IV. It makes no sense to draw harsh, marker-like lines. For a natural look, use pencil liners instead of liquid liners.

10. Mascara Mistakes

First things first, you must use a mascara that is two shades darker than your eyebrow color. Never apply more than two coats of mascara, or your eyelashes will end up looking extremely clumpy. Mascara that is three to four months old also results in clumping of your lashes.

Don't use mascara on your lower lashes the same way you apply on your upper lashes. It will clump up and give your spider leg lashes. Instead, hold the wand vertically and apply.

Waterproof mascara is obviously amazing, and it's most likely that you will be inclined to invest in one, and use only that. But, it is not a very good idea. Waterproof mascara is much harder to remove, and its application and removal could seriously affect your lashes. Your lashes may wither away sooner. If you must use waterproof mascara, make sure you do it only during the summer months.

11. Bronzer Blunders

A bronzer is not meant to be swept all over the canvas of your face. Avoid using too much bronzer. The idea of a bronzer is to use it exactly where the sun would naturally hit your face. Make sure you apply your bronzer only on your cheekbones, the top of your forehead, and the jawline. If you are doing it right, you will notice that you are actually drawing the number 3 on both the sides of your face.

12. Lip Liner Woes

Harsh lip lines while doing your makeup is the worst thing you can do to yourself. Do not draw a thin sharp line on your lips to outline them. It is one of the biggest peeves. Also, your lips can end up looking weird if you have chosen a dark liner with a lighter lipstick shade. They are meant to define your lips and not to create a border line around them.

You wear a lip liner to keep your lipstick from bleeding. If you draw a harsh outline, it will tend to fade away, making your lips look terrible. The idea is to blend well. Draw a smudged outline, almost like you are shading your lips with the pencil, for best results. Another correct technique is to draw the outline and then fill in your entire lips with a lip liner that suits your lipstick shade and then go over it with the lipstick. This will help you avoid a lipstick on teeth situation.

13. Tacky Lipstick Color

A lipstick can make or break your look. Stick to colors that are natural and suit your skin tone. Dark shades can look tacky. They also make you look much older than you are. If you do go in for dark colors, make sure the rest of your makeup is light.

14. Face Powder Fetish

Face powder seems like the perfect makeup finale to lock it all up, and keep the shine at bay. But, it can also make you look aged. Believe it or not, face powder emphasizes fine lines and wrinkles. It is best to use it only on your T-zone, and try to avoid it completely as you age.

15. Clown Cheeks

Without proper application, blush can make you look like a clown. Whenever putting on blush, use foundation. Otherwise, the color becomes too hard on your cheeks. And make sure to swirl the brush in the product, tap off excess and then apply on your face. Otherwise, you will pick up too much product and end up looking overdone.

16. Highlight At The Wrong Places

Do not apply a single eyeshadow color to your entire eye area, as they may give you racoon eyes. Always use a highlighter shade to enhance your brow bone. Golden or silver highlighters will compliment all the shades under the sun.

17. Flashy Fingernails

Long, flashy fingernails don't always give the best impression. They can look witchy and claw-like. Always keep your nails neatly groomed.

18. Dry Shampoo Distress

Dry shampoo is probably one of the best inventions yet. For those of you who don't know what it is, it involves putting dry powder on your scalp such that it absorbs all the oil.

Here's how to do it right.

You must wait for the powder to absorb all the oil. So, in effect, it takes a while for the dry shampoo to do its job. Do not get impatient. You can use a dry shampoo immediately after you wash your hair. Using it immediately after a shampoo will help your hair stay fresher for a longer time. Do not spray it too close to your hair. Holding it six inches away while you are spraying is ideal.

You need to wash your hair after one or two uses of the dry shampoo, else the chemical build-up will make your hair look dull and dry.

19. Perfume Overload

One spray of perfume is all it takes to make you smell like a dream. Too much perfume, however, can be offensive. It is very easy to get carried away with perfume, but overdoing it can cause allergies and headaches. A body mist is less concentrated and is a better option.

20. Sleeping With Makeup On

There are absolutely no excuses for going to bed without removing all traces of makeup. To keep your skin healthy, make sure you remove the makeup before you go to sleep. Failing to do so will make your skin dry and prone to acne and infections.

21. Sleeping On Your Side

A supine position is not only good for your back, but it also helps avoid lines and wrinkles on your skin which can develop if you sleep on your side. It might take a little practice to make it a habit of sleeping on your back.

22. Entangled Beauty Trends

Either play up your eyes or your lips. Too much makeup on both will make you look unsightly. If you are wearing bright/smokey eye makeup, go for pale, nude, or natural-looking lipsticks. If you are wearing loud shades on your lips, go for natural, slight eyeliner and lots of mascara.

23. Matching Your Makeup With Your Clothes

Matching is old-school, and in no way classic vintage. When your clothes are bright and so is your makeup, it only spells tacky. Makeup artists believe that if your clothes are vibrant, you should go for a neutral palette makeup-wise. If you pick a metallic wardrobe to dazzle through the holidays, make sure you avoid glossy cosmetics and stick to the ever-so-classic smokey eye.

24. Too Much Glitter Is Not Gold

Shimmer is fun, and it sets the ambiance for the festivities. But not if you looked like you smeared your face with glue and dipped it in glitter. That is just a big NO.

25. Playing Up Both The Eyes And The Lips

You either let your eyes dazzle or glam up your lips. It has to be one or the other, and not both. If you are going gung-ho with your eye makeup, keep your lips nude or neutral, and if your lips are stealing the thunder, keep your eye makeup natural. Or else, you will be summoning disaster.

26. Smearing Lipstick Until It Starts To Bleed

Lipstick is lovely, but that doesn't mean that you need to touch it up every time you visit the bathroom. After a point, it will start to look messy, and then you will hardly be able to tell where your lip line begins and where it ends. Touch up, but be aware of how it looks.

27. Omitting The Primer

Primers have been around for a while, but women are beginning to use them only now. You might spend all your time perfecting your makeup but unless you have a primer, the chaos of the party will either cause your makeup to bleed or fade, or your face will look like you have just taken a dip in oil and posed. To keep your makeup intact for a fair period of time, and to look flash-ready all the time, it is best you use a primer before you apply your makeup.

28. A Runny Eye

Girls just want to have fun, and when you are all caught up in the heat of the night, dancing away to glory, you might not notice that bleeding eyeshadow. The best way to ensure you look as fresh as a daisy even at 2am is to use an eyeshadow primer.

29. Trusting A Friend Who Is "GOOD" At Makeup

The Secrets of Beauty

Yes, she is your best friend, and you don't want to hurt her. But if she doesn't know makeup, don't let her touch your face. Not even if the celebrations have made you woozy.

The Secrets of Beauty

CHAPTER 9

SELF-CARE FOR BEAUTY AND WELL BEING

Self care is so diverse and versatile. Activities that simply involve your day-to-day skincare or makeup organization count as self care. These self care activities fall under the beauty self care category. When you look great, you also feel great. Beauty self care can be very relaxing and simple. A face mask can do so much for your skin after a long day or a facial massage can make your face feel much better right after waking up.

This I will dive into beauty self care ideas like skincare, hair, general hygiene, and makeup that you can add to your self care routine to make it feel special.

The Secrets of Beauty

What is beauty self-care?

Beauty self care involves **taking care of your skin, hair, and mindset towards beauty and overall outer appearance and welling.** This kind of self-care is not meant to be superficial but meant for you to take care of your outer body and appearance. How you take care of your appearance also affects how you feel.

Doing self care and taking good care of yourself will eventually improve how you look and how you feel about yourself.

Beauty Self Care Ideas To Make You Feel and Look Better

1. Take a warm shower or bath

The Secrets of Beauty

One of the simplest beauty self care ideas you can do is to take a long relaxing warm shower or bath. Not only will you be able to whine down, but also hydrate and moisturize your skin. Some items you can include are bath bombs, flower petals, or even have a wireless speaker to play relaxing spa music.

2. Wash your hair

Haircare is also self care. No matter what your hair type, texture, or color, you will need to wash your hair. The simple act of washing your hair is enough to count as self care. To make it more special, you can add hair masks or try a new style. Washing day for my natural hair is a self care activity that I do every week or I pay someone to do it for me. I have a lot of hair, so it's less of a hassle. Sometimes it's better for me to have a professional take care of it and advise me what to do to keep my hair healthy or what to improve on.

3. Do a face mask

Give your skin a nice hydration boost or a nice glow with a face mask. This is a classic self care idea that I recommend in every kind of self care article I've written from quick self care ideas to even winter self care. Face masks can be either bought premade in a store like Ulta or you can try a DIY recipe. I recommend finding one that your skin will like and not react to because as someone with acne-prone skin, I know that some masks won't work with my skin.

My favorite brands of face masks include the TonyMoly face masks and the Crème Shop and BT21 collaborations. Both are Korean skincare, so the ingredients are better and work better (for my skin at least). **BT21's Face Masks** come and go at Ulta and have been re-released from time to time. I recommend going to a K-pop store to see if they have any in stock. When I say that these are the best masks I've used, I mean it.

4. Exfoliate your skin

One of my favorite beauty self care activities is exfoliating my skin. Since I have dry and sensitive skin, I have to exfoliate often to prevent my pores from clogging and breaking out. I recommend that you find out what your skin type is to know when to exfoliate your skin.

I personally LOVE this Secret Key Lemon Sparkling Peeling Gel that reveals your dead skin cells and exfoliates without being harsh on your skin. It's really cool and a little gross for some people. It's also Korean skincare.

5. Clean your makeup brushes

You know those makeup brushes that have been sitting in your makeup bag or makeup cart…for weeks? Please clean them!

My skin changed when I finally took the time to clean my makeup brushes. My skin stopped breaking out so badly whenever I wore makeup.

This is self care for sure. You have no idea how much bacteria is growing or sitting on your makeup brushes. It's important that you wash your brushes to prevent them from spreading. Cleaning them is also kind of therapeutic.

Also, leave the DIY makeup cleaning recipes on Pinterest and leave your hair shampoo alone. I used to do all of them in high school and early college. It honestly was a waste of products and probably led to more break outs for me.

6. Organize your makeup and other beauty-related products

Another beauty self care idea you can do on a chill day is to organize your makeup. Take some time to figure out what makeup products you can toss and keep. This also makes the process of finding what you need when you apply your makeup easier. If you have space in your bedroom or bathroom, I also recommend investing in a makeup cart organizer.

This is a life hack that changed how cluttered my bathroom was and had all my beauty supplies in one spot.

7. Shave (if you do so)

Depending on the mood, shaving can feel like a chore or a therapeutic activity. But procrastinating on shaving can make it even worse. As part of your beauty self care routine, take the time to understand how to shave your body better such as buying the correct razors, what to do to your skin to make it easier, and the aftercare. I honestly have put up a white flag and am in the process of getting laser hair removal for my armpits. Shaving was so painful and difficult with my armpits over the last few years. So far, after one treatment, it's amazing.

8. Get your eyebrows waxed or trimmed

Eyebrows are important! Taking time to get them trimmed or waxed can be part of your beauty self care. I also recommend going to a professional to understand how to frame your eyebrows and make it less of a hassle. Trust me, all those YouTube videos I watched as a teen just made the skin around my eyebrows mad and red and did not help shape my eyebrows.

9. Visit a local spa for a facial

Facials have several benefits outside of relaxation like anti-aging, tailored skin care, and doing whitehead and blackhead extractions safely. Book an appointment with an esthetician for a facial can be part of your self care!

10. Get a manicure or pedicure

A classic self care idea that you can do any weekend. Get a manicure or pedicure. Manicures help your nails from growing hangnails, dry skin, and much more. Overall, it helps promote healthy nails.

I recently started getting pedicures because my family recommended that I just go with them and now I like going to my local nail salon/spa. But getting a pedicure is a relaxing activity. Depending on the salon, they will exfoliate, moisture your legs, and of course, paint them.

11. Straighten or curl your hair

If you want to change up your hairstyle, then straighten or curl it. Remember to use heat protection to keep your hair from getting damaged!

12. Wear sunscreen

Sunscreen is probably one of the most important beauty/skincare products that we need to wear every day. Sunscreen also helps slow down aging, protects layers of your skin, prevents skin-related diseases, and much more. Adding sunscreen to your skincare routine is one of the best beauty self care ideas you can do. My to-go sunscreen nowadays is the EltaMD UV Daily SPF 40 Tinted Sunscreen. It was recommended by my dermatologist since I had hypopigmentation and was using a lot of retinoids.

13. Deep condition your hair

Deep conditioning your hair can work wonders. Add this step to your hair routine to add more hydration. There are several deep conditioners out there, depending on your hair type and texture.

14. Brush your teeth with extra care

Taking care of our teeth is important. Your teeth's health can tell you about many things and not taking care of your teeth can lead to several health issues. Take the extra step to brush your teeth longer twice a day and floss and pay attention while doing it.

15. Give your face a massage

A new beauty self care that I've been doing on and off is face massages. I don't have a rose quartz facial roller or anything special for it. But I just use my hands and massage my face. This honestly changed the way my face felt when I was stuffy and helped me wake up in the morning.

16. Take a trip to Sephora or Ulta

A trip to Ulta or Sephora is relaxing, especially if the store isn't busy. Taking your time looking at beauty products and learning something new is cool. Another beauty self care idea that I recommend is going into Ulta and asking the sales associate to help you find the best foundation, blush, etc. they have in the store. Or even schedule Ulta's hair salon or with their makeup artists.

17. Find beauty within you and define it

The Secrets of Beauty

The last beauty self care idea I have is to reflect or journal about beauty to find the beauty inside of you. We are constantly told what beauty is and what it is not. But beauty trends come and go. It's best to find the beauty inside of you and what you find beautiful. Create your own beauty standards and embrace them. Love your beauty and take care of it!

What is self care and well being?

Self-care means taking the time to do things that help you live well and improve both your physical health and mental health. When it comes to your mental health, self-care can help you manage stress, lower your risk of illness, and increase your energy. Even small acts of self-care in your daily life can have a big impact.

Here are some tips to help you get started with self-care:

1. **Get regular exercise.** Just 30 minutes of walking every day can help boost your

mood and improve your health. Small amounts of exercise add up, so don't be discouraged if you can't do 30 minutes at one time.

II. **Eat healthy**, regular meals and stay hydrated. A balanced diet and plenty of water can improve your energy and focus throughout the day. Also, limit caffeinated beverages such as soft drinks or coffee.

III. **Make sleep a priority.** Stick to a schedule, and make sure you're getting enough sleep. Blue light from devices and screens can make it harder to fall asleep, so reduce blue light exposure from your phone or computer before bedtime.

IV. **Try a relaxing activity**. Explore relaxation or wellness programs or apps, which may incorporate meditation, muscle relaxation, or breathing exercises. Schedule regular times for these and other healthy activities you enjoy such as journaling.

V.   **Set goals and priorities**. Decide what must get done now and what can wait. Learn to say "no" to new tasks if you start to feel like you're taking on too much. Try to be mindful of what you have accomplished at the end of the day, not what you have been unable to do.

VI.   **Practice gratitude**. Remind yourself daily of things you are grateful for. Be specific. Write them down at night, or replay them in your mind.

VII.   **Focus on positivity**. Identify and challenge your negative and unhelpful thoughts.

VIII.   **Stay connected**. Reach out to your friends or family members who can provide emotional support and practical help.

Self-care looks different for everyone, and it is important to find what you need and enjoy. It may take trial and error to discover what works best for you. In addition, although self-care is not a cure for mental illnesses, understanding what causes or triggers your mild symptoms and what coping techniques work for you can help manage your mental health.

How do I take care of myself to look beautiful?

Are you tired of spending hours in front of the mirror wondering how to look beautiful naturally? This book is for you. Read further to find out tips and techniques to appear beautiful every day and naturally.

Here are some ways that one can look naturally beautiful:

1. Regularly Moisturize Your Skin

Moisturisation is crucial for your hydration. Apply a good moisturizer daily that suits your skin. It will keep your skin soft and supple.

2. Get Beauty Sleep

Sleep deprivation can make you look tired and develop dark circles around your eyes. It is because the lack of sleep dilates the blood vessels.

Sufficient sleep lowers stress and gives you better skin. It also helps you to get rid of those dark circles. Getting at least eight hours of uninterrupted sleep is crucial for maintaining skin health.

You can also buy a sleeping mask that will block all the lights to get better-uninterrupted sleep.

3. Drink Enough Water

Water has amazing benefits not only for your health but also for your skin. Drinking enough water helps you flush the toxins out of your system and keep your skin hydrated and conditioned from within. It clears out your skin and makes it appear radiant. Water will help treat acne and other skin problems. It also maintains a healthy supply of oxygen in the body, which, in turn, helps to keep your skin glowing. It also reduces the risk of premature aging, fine lines, wrinkles, and puffiness. You should drink 8-10 glasses of water every day to improve your skin's elasticity. Keep a bottle with you to avoid dehydration. You can also have green tea, fruit juices, and more to increase your water content.

4. Pluck Your Eyebrows

Properly plucked eyebrows enhance your beauty. Get a good set of tweezers and get your eyebrows cleaned up. Having eyebrows perfectly plucked can make your whole face look great.

5. Exercise Regularly

Apart from keeping you fit and healthy, regular exercise is beneficial for the skin. You should work out for the skin because it helps improve blood circulation, which delivers essential vitamins and nutrients to your face and makes it appear healthy and glowing.

This is crucial for treating acne and other oxidative damage on the skin. Therefore, you should develop a habit of exercising consistently to look pretty naturally.

6. Use Sunscreen Every Day

The long wave ultraviolet A (UVA) and short wave ultraviolet B (UVB) are harmful sun rays. These rays, especially UVA, can penetrate deep into the dermis, the thickest layer of skin, and damage your skin. The rays cause premature aging, sunspots and may also lead to serious skin problems such as skin cancer. Therefore, it is necessary to wear broad-spectrum sunscreen every day before stepping out in the sun. Skin dermatologists recommend that you should wear at least SPF 30 sunscreen. SPF is the sun protection factor determining how well the sunscreen will protect you. Choose a sunscreen for your skin type and apply it regularly.

7. Drink Green Tea

Besides being a drink for weight loss, green tea is rich in antioxidants and benefits the skin. Its detoxifying properties flush toxins out of your body, improve gut health, and reduce skin issues. You should at least have two cups of green tea every day to naturally get clear and beautiful skin.

CONCLUSION

As you embark on your journey to discover the best beauty routine for you, remember that true beauty comes from within. It's not just about the products you use or the techniques you master - it's about feeling comfortable and confident in your own skin. Be kind to yourself, experiment with different looks and products, and have fun with it. After all, beauty should be a source of joy and self-expression, not a source of stress or insecurity.

Listen, the most important thing to remember is this: you're already beautiful, inside and out. This book is here to help you find the right products and techniques to bring out your inner beauty and make you feel amazing. But always remember that your worth isn't defined by your appearance. You're awesome just the way you are. Now go out there and rock your unique style!